L.E.A.D.

Learning
Education
Action
Destiny

52 Leadership Lessons That Last a Lifetime

Glen Aubrey

www.Lead52.com
www.CreativeTeamPublishing.com

Creative Team Publishing
San Diego

© 2008 by Glen Aubrey
All rights reserved. No part of this book may be reproduced, stored in a retrieval system, or transmitted in any form or by any means without the prior written permission of the publisher, except by a reviewer who may quote brief passages in a review to be printed in a newspaper, magazine, or journal.

First Printing

ISBN: 978-0-9797358-2-0
PUBLISHED BY CREATIVE TEAM PUBLISHING
www.CreativeTeamPublishing.com
San Diego

Printed in the United States of America

L.E.A.D.

Learning
Education
Action
Destiny

52 Leadership Lessons That Last a Lifetime

Glen Aubrey

www.Lead52.com
www.CreativeTeamPublishing.com

You are making decisions for a lifetime not yet recorded.
—Michell Cook, M.T.S.

Dedication

When I was very young, my family was served by a physician by the name of Doctor Hoover. His medical suite was located in downtown San Diego, in a charming old home next door to my dad's business on Sixth Avenue. A small fish pond occupied a conspicuous place in his immaculately kept front yard. Flowering plants bordered the curved entry path. A palm tree provided shade. The small, one-story house was warm and welcoming.

Dr. Hoover was elderly when I knew him. His methods were old-fashioned and effective. My grandmother often went to see him, and she highly respected him. My parents and I trusted him, too.

One of my vivid memories of Dr. Hoover is that he kept a skeleton in his closet—literally. The model skeleton was adult-sized, and he would use it to help his patients understand human anatomy, pinpointing problematic areas relative to the patient's condition.

The "skeleton in the closet" is an expression that usually means covering up truth or hiding a secret past. But in the doctor's case, the skeleton in the closet was an educational tool; Dr. Hoover wanted his patients to learn about their conditions. He recognized that with knowledge, solutions to medical problems could be more clearly understood, appreciated, and applied.

Skeleton truths may reside in studies of leadership, too. Call them frameworks, foundational facts, or primary principles, they are structures every living team organism should learn and educate others about. Effective teams build action and chart destiny upon them.

One job of the leader is to put flesh on these bones, to build a body of practices so the entire entity becomes a living, breathing model of desired motivations and behaviors. This may not be an easy task, but it is a necessary one in constructing great teams made of maturing people. *L.E.A.D.—Learning, Education, Action, Destiny* is written for leaders and teams who desire to take enduring principles—the staple skeleton of truths—and mold them into strong and enduring practices.

This body requires organs, sinews, and connecting ligaments if a being is to come alive and create positive contributions. A team's Values, Vision, Mission, and Message are their essence. Together these compose their Code of Achievement, their DNA (see pages 29-34). The leader's job is to help followers grow their organism from a skeleton of principles into a functioning and contributing body of practices where their Code of Achievement becomes their life.

Turning concept into consistent action presents opportunities and challenges. Chances for growth and improvement require changes in reception and reaction from willing leaders and earnest followers. Lessons learned become practices lived when teachers and students receive and act upon enduring truths.

If you're the leader building an effective team, or the doctor helping a team diagnose their ills and applying healing remedies, or a follower who desires long lasting improvements, then this book is dedicated to you. Use it in cooperation with the three prior business publications, listed on page 18, which compose a business life investment model of positive relationships and excellent functions.

Take yourself, your team, and your networks to higher levels of health. Make the commitment not to hide skeleton truths in the closet of your mind, but instead to adorn this framework with flesh, feelings, tangible contributions, and futures of maturing people who provision well.

After decades passed between childhood and young adulthood, I found myself looking for a downtown business address for my own company and chanced to drive by the doctor's old house. By that time, it had been converted on the inside to several small offices, but the outside of the building had retained its charm.

Upon investigation, I learned that one office was vacant and available for occupancy. This small one-desk area was almost certainly a room where the skeleton had been stored by Dr. Hoover. I rented this office immediately. What had been the space to house an educational tool became the place to create curriculum designed to help core teams succeed. A closet for a model became a place of model-making, where principles and practices were framed, and foundations of building and implementing teams were formed.

Unfortunately, that historical home with its quaint gardens and quiet fish pond are long gone now. The attractive and charming structure was torn down and replaced by a parking lot many years ago.

But special memories remain of its former days. So do the motives and meaning of enduring truths, combined into curriculum that students embrace today. I am one who, as a child, witnessed a closeted skeleton that was used to teach people understanding. I am also one who, as a leader and trainer, endeavors to bring lessons of learning, education, action, and destiny to eager students in the workplace.

These students desire to know, grow, and apply what they learn. They compose great teams. They cooperate and produce excellence. I am one of them, most of all.

This book is for the learner in all of us. Let's grow together.

Description

L.E.A.D.—Learning, Education, Action, Destiny is a compilation of 52 leadership lessons designed to present leadership principles in practical application, one lesson for each week of the year. A study guide for *L.E.A.D.*, entitled *Leadership Works*, promotes advance study. Both the book and study guide are available for purchase on-line at **www.Lead52.com** and through the Creative Team Resources Group (CTRG) online store, **www.ctrg.com**.

Permissions and Credits

Opening quotation used with permission of Michell Cook, M.T.S.

Quotations from *Leadership Is— How To Build Your Legacy,* originally published by PublishAmerica, © 2005, used with permission of PublishAmerica.

Quotations from *Industrial Strength Solutions Build Successful Work Teams!,* originally published by PublishAmerica, © 2006, used with permission of PublishAmerica.

Word definitions from *Merriam Webster's 11th Collegiate Dictionary.*

Table of Contents

Dedication
Description
Permissions and Credits
Opening 17
Lessons 25
    1 Initiative 27
    2 Values 29
    3 Vision, Mission, and Message 33
    4 A Value System 35
    5 Leaders Are Followers First 39
    6 Praise 41
    7 Decisions 43
    8 Business Growth 45
    9 Agreement 49
    10 Character Is Revealed When Conflict Comes 51
    11 Conflict Resolution 53
    12 Frameworks 57
    13 Investment 59
    14 Interaction 61
    15 Relationship and Function 63
    16 The Storehouse of Giving 65
    17 Celebrations 69
    18 Seven-Step Process of Solution Provision—
        Dealing With Incidents and Issues 71
    19 A Core Team Leader's Responsibilities 77
    20 Close the Loops 83
    21 Thankfulness 85
    22 Success Through Mentoring 87
    23 Nurture and Support 89

24 Engaged Leadership—The Process of Connecting 91
25 Creating Workplace Positives. 93
26 Recognizing and Pursuing Personal Opportunity. 95
27 Integrity. 99
28 Great People and Great Production 101
29 Rewarding Achievement 103
30 Interdependence 105
31 The Essence of Great Leadership. 107
32 Change Is Challenging. 111
33 A Fresh Perspective. 113
34 Reflections. 117
35 Goals 121
36 Restoring Relationships on a Team 123
37 Emerging Leadership, Building People—It's Not New . . 125
38 It's All About Details 129
39 Leaders Communicate 133
40 It's About Time 135
41 Planning. 139
42 Profit Centers 141
43 Principles in Practice—Where Rubber Meets Road. . . . 145
44 Without Decisive Action, It's Worthless 147
45 Absentee Leadership 151
46 When Followers Take Initiative 155
47 Leading From the Middle. 157
48 Problem Solving Techniques 159
49 How Leaders Handle Discouragement 163
50 Winning or Whining—What Do You Encourage?. 167
51 Opportunities for Leadership Come From
    Circumstances and They Are Created 169
52 You Are More Important Than What You Do 171
Closing 175

Acknowledgements. 177
Creative Team Resources Group (CTRG) 181
The Author. 183
The Publisher. 185
Products. 186

Opening

Let's define several key terms and a foundational principle used in *L.E.A.D.—Learning, Education, Action, Destiny*. At Creative Team Resources Group, Inc. (**CTRG, www.ctrg.com**) we use the words *relationship* and *function* consistently, as well as *Core Team*. Here are their meanings:

- *Relationship* is defined as the decision one makes about the success of another.
- *Function* is defined as the task that proves the validity of the decision.
- *Core Team* describes a group of growing individuals who work together based on these structural, relational, and functional foundations:

  C—Consistency in relationships and functions

  O—Obedience to core values

  R—Right relationships that endure

  E—Example, where the question is not if one has an example, but "What kind of example does he or she have?"

  T—Trust offered freely when a relationship begins and proven over time as a relationship extends

  E—Essentials of composite nature, comprising experience, education, and environment

  A—Accountability, "...repeatable proof over time that a person and his or her performance can be counted upon, that consistent results will accompany the process of endeavor." (From *Core Teams Work*, page 102, see below.)

M—Methods, functions and contributions performed with excellence

The single and unalterable premise upon which we frame our teachings and practices is this: People are more important than production and relationship precedes and gives birth to function.

These truths and their definitions are essential to understanding the concepts and associated applications referenced throughout this book. They also resonate within three prior books:

- *Leadership Is— How to Build Your Legacy (***www.LeadershipIs.com***)*
- *Industrial Strength Solutions Build Successful Work Teams! (***www.IndustrialStrengthSolutions.com***)*
- *Core Teams Work Their Principles and Practices (***www.CoreTeamsWork.com***)*

You are invited to refer to these books as you go through this volume, to enhance learning and encourage remembrance as you embrace what you read.

Embark on a journey of life and leadership discovery. Climb the mountain of principled truth. Delve eagerly into learning, education, and action. When you do, you create a process of growth, a destiny for yourself and those who follow.

Take the lessons you observe on the page and make them the

actions you purposefully engage. Positive results emerge over time in your life and the lives of those you impact.

Learning

Great teachers are dedicated students. Great leaders are committed followers. These teachers and leaders impart lessons they are convinced are true and worthy of application. They invest into the lives of those who look to them for information and example.

A quest for learning is insatiable in the heart of the eager student. People who want to mature express little contentment for the status quo of what they know. They want more.

How do you learn? When most groups we work with are asked this question, the usual replies reference learning from mistakes. Have you considered how often you learn from victories and successes as well? Both sources are important in a balanced learning process.

If there were an outline of effective learning techniques, what would it look like? Consider this one:
1. Teacher and student discover their interconnecting points, the common threads of interest and application that bring them together. They agree on basic principles, the values they both believe are immovable. Their agreements promote conceptual receptivity and practical use of what they learn.

2. Teacher and student develop cooperative relationships and functions. The teacher makes a great decision about the success of the student, taking time and supplying tools to help the student grasp, retain, and act on truth. The student makes a great decision about the teacher's success (as well as his or her own) when the student learns well, is grateful for the instruction, thanks the teacher, and diligently applies learning in his or her environments.
3. Teacher and student willfully consider varied perspectives as they pursue discovery of truth. Open communication and forthright discussion foster atmospheres of thoughtful inquiry and purposeful decision making.
4. Teacher and student consistently evaluate growth in their processes of learning and achievement. They chart courses for continual quests to learn more. They assure that information imparted and received is practiced in life.

Leadership Is— describes the Course of Attainment beginning on page 173. There are five states of the course: Dreams, Desires, Goals, Action, and Reality. Learning is about moving from dreams toward reality. Learners set goals, act on them, evaluate progress, correct errors, and celebrate successes. They design and improve methods of growth. They expand their knowledge and use wisdom in application. People who learn, mature.

Whether you are leading or following, educating or learning, you remain a diligent student of principle and practice when you earnestly seek information and use it to build up the members of your team. Learning individuals attract others of like passion. They compose a group of dedicated people on a core team. Regardless of title, tenure, position, or station, the one who learns educates others for mutual benefits. Processes of learning never cease for members of a core team who desire strong relationships and consistent functions.

Education

Leaders are eager to impart truth to receptive followers. Educators long to see the success of their instruction in changed behaviors of those they reach and teach.

Education is the act of imparting knowledge into receptive hearts and minds. Great teachers educate their students because they want to see them to grow.

Students and followers are served well when teachers and leaders present meaningful information. Learners are served best when wisdom accompanies that instruction. Wisdom is the understanding of how to use information well. Knowledge without wisdom does not profit anyone who possesses information but fails to apply it appropriately. The most effective instructors teach information and the methods to put it into life.

A great educator instills designs for duplication into the minds and motions of those who are taught. This leader, by expression and example, expects that his or her followers will one day become instructors themselves. So they model the behaviors they want their students to emulate. They plan their content and methods to best fit the needs and aspirations of the learners.

Education is readily available. There is simply no limit to the sources and courses on virtually any topic of interest. The key is to find or create the right teaching methods and tools that work most effectively for teacher and student, leader and follower.

An educator who cares more is one who relies less on dusty, worn out, and moldy instructional methods that may not resonate with a student. A teacher who views education holistically employs fresher and fuller means of imparting truth, *so that the experiences of education are as valuable as the information shared within them.*

Education should not be confined within edifices of brick and mortar. Indeed, classrooms may be completely unorthodox. Innovative minds formulate and encourage creative methods to educate eager learners.

Inspiration and encouragement well up from the heart of a teacher who truly wants the best for the ones who are learning. Think of educators who have inspired you and how they did it. What methods characterized their education styles?

A dedicated instructor considers multiple means of educating. He or she chooses techniques that assure receptivity and work for the greatest results.

Action

Changed and improved behaviors are abiding proofs of effective learning and education. Action and production are natural results of information instilled into ready minds, then distilled into patterns of living.

If action doesn't occur, communication and learning are not complete. Those who learn much and educate well expect to observe positive behavioral changes in teachers and students, leaders and followers.

Action, of course, is doing something, not just thinking about it. Ideas remain concepts until a person acts.

Behaviors are demonstrations of effective learning and education. What a person does shows just how much they've taken in and how much they'll give back again.

Put another way, action is function emerging from solid relationships. A decision to learn all one can and educate those who want to grow (relationship) is seen when an instructor helps others achieve their dreams and goals (function). This is success.

Destiny

Learning, education, and action create models of engagement. Together they provide proof tests of accountability and endurance. These proof tests are the elements of destiny.

Destiny constitutes a conclusion of a process, but it is also made up of the process itself. Think of destiny not only as a consequence but as the means of achieving desired ends.

Great leaders never stop learning. They never cease to educate eager followers. Their actions, based on what they receive and give, form frameworks of investment where benefits are shared from one generation to the next.

The journey is the destination, a part of creating a living legacy. Destiny combines learning, education, action, and results. Who you are and who you become constitute living proofs of positive outcomes, seen in the lives of those you touch.

Lessons

L.E.A.D.—Learning, Education, Action, Destiny can be utilized in several effective ways.

- Individuals use the book and *Leadership Works*, its companion study guide, for personal study and application. The book and study guide are available at **www.Lead52.com**.
- Teams use the book and the study guide as curriculum at weekly staff meetings, covering one lesson each week of the year.

Take the book and its study guide and make them your own. Chart your progress. Celebrate your success! Let's begin.

Lesson 1
Initiative

Leadership is present when the one in charge takes initiative. Without initiative a leadership vacuum exists. No excuses—innovation, creativity, and activity replace complacency, whining, and mediocrity. The person who doesn't live in the latter will lead in the former.

Understanding what to do, how to do it, and the realistic expectations of results when proper initiative is applied are parts of a leader's quest for winning. Changes of behavior are required. They start with the leader.

Leaders who want improvements do something, set the pace, and forge the paths. They act. They substitute wallowing in less than desirable circumstances with positive actions born of winning attitudes.

Initiative is a mindset and a must for greater accomplishments and growth in worthwhile endeavors. It may be a natural or learned trait of exceptional leaders.

Initiative stands for the right, anchored on core values shared with those who will be impacted by the leader's choices of behavior. Actions of worth and worthy of praise are focused on positive results. Contributions promote the good that values intend. Consider, initiate, engage, and lead.

L.E.A.D. — LEARNING, EDUCATION, ACTION, DESTINY

Lesson 2
Values

Leaders fashion principle-driven frameworks into which followers contribute and from which leaders and followers grow. These frameworks are structures founded on values. Values are the principles upon which leaders and followers agree. They are rock solid, unmoved by circumstances and winds of change. Actions based on shared values result in stability, accountability, endurance, and personal growth, ensuring meaningful relationships.

What are the values of your core team? How well do your followers know them and how often do they refer to them? How much do you and your followers share full agreement on their definitions and applications?

View an example of primary tenets, the Values, Vision, Mission, and Message of Creative Team Resources Group, Inc. (CTRG), along with the company's Value System, on pages 31 and 32. The collection of Values, Vision, Mission, and Message is called the Code of Achievement (from *Leadership Is—*, pages 52-54).

Designate your list of values. Define each one clearly. Seek agreement from your followers on all of them. Ratify them. Articulate them often. Strive to live them out. Lead with them. Show those who look to you for leadership how important these values are through your declaration and example. (Please see *Core Teams Work*, pages 161-163, for a list of core values you may wish to consider for your team. Or use this list to stimulate your thinking to identify others unique to your work environment.)

L.E.A.D. — LEARNING, EDUCATION, ACTION, DESTINY

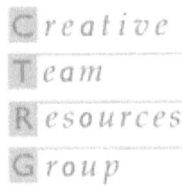

www.ctrg.com * www.LeadershipIs.com * www.IndustrialStrengthSolutions.com
www.CoreTeamsWork.com * www.Lead52.com

Values, Vision, Mission, Message
Creative Team Resources Group, Inc.
Copyright 2005 Creative Team Resources Group, Inc., CTRG

Values:

1. Integrity: Truth in word and deed
2. Authenticity: Words and deeds that match
3. Relationships: Decisions about another's success
4. Functional Excellence: Proofs of our relationships
5. Modeling: Duplication into other's lives
6. Legacy: Greater works from our followers
7. Accountability: Completion and closure
8. Enjoyment: Celebration of people and process
9. Rewards: Intangible and tangible results of our efforts
10. Experience: Full engagement on the journey of growth

Vision: To see lives and organizations changed for the better.

Mission: We provide great information that encourages people to make better decisions about how they live and work, and we do this through building Core Teams.

Message: People are more important than what they do.

GLEN AUBREY

www.ctrg.com * www.LeadershipIs.com * www.IndustrialStrengthSolutions.com
www.CoreTeamsWork.com * www.Lead52.com

Value System
Creative Team Resources Group, Inc.
Copyright 2005 Creative Team Resources Group, Inc., CTRG

Value System:

The Twelve Laws of Understanding:

1. Realize I am responsible for my own choices, not others'; that changing someone else's behavior is not my responsibility; rather, I need to change me.
2. Seek to understand how the other person thinks and communicates; use his or her language.
3. Model what I want.
4. Set realistic limits on what is acceptable behavior.
5. Impose these limits on myself, first.
6. Desire the best, but prepare for difficulty; seek creative, peaceful solutions.
7. Seek and pray for wisdom.
8. Remember, at the right times.
9. Encourage always.
10. Think first, listen most, and speak seldom.
11. Realize growth involves change, change can mean pain, and patience on the journey is a virtue.
12. Love. Establish meaningful relationships.

Lesson 3
Vision, Mission, and Message

Many organizations confuse the meanings of Vision, Mission, and Message. Let's clarify these terms.

Vision is why an entity exists. Vision provides reasons behind a group's actions, identifying motives and providing motivation. Vision creates expectations in organizational change for the better.

Mission is what an organization does and the methods it utilizes to accomplish its tasks. Mission defines dedicated endeavors and expected results. When team members cooperate to fulfill their mission, they encourage one another to create best-deliverables in personal growth and customer service provision.

In combination with Values, Vision and Mission provide frameworks of continuity for an organization that seeks to fulfill its goals in cooperation with its unchangeable principled foundations. If you are the leader, consider your Vision. Why does your organization exist? Clearly articulate your company's Mission with your team.

Then look closely at *Message*. Your message is composed of the life-changing lessons you and your group learn and teach to the targets you want to reach.

How do you and your group desire to be remembered? What lessons do your examples of principled practice teach, and to whom? Your answers will help you decide on the contents and targets of your message.

Lesson 4
A Value System

Refer to page 38. Consider the merits of constructing a Value System. In *Leadership Is—*, the following explanation is given on pages 105 and 106:

"A leader's expectations of a follower and a follower's expectations of a leader share common values: concrete fundamental principles of life beliefs and living practices. A value system is a collection of these core values, but the system is more than a list. In aggregate the core values form a composite framework of principles that taken holistically provide measurements against which atmospheres, attitudes and actions can be evaluated as to how they measure up in practice and outcomes when compared to the standards of the system.

"A value system integrates right principles with right practices in the assurance that empowered and changed behaviors will produce better and more positive results. Principles, processes and production (motive, means and ends) are all considered and weighed within a value system. The system is dynamic in that while it is based on unchanging truths, it continually adjusts its means according to the needs of the culture in which it is applied (work, family, and social environments). The system is resoundingly strong, resilient in nature, responsible in practice, but not rigid in method.

"A value system when operational empowers a leader and follower to grow while they are engaged in the practices of their investment. It is vital that both leader and follower are committed to fulfilling and abiding by the core values to which they willfully commit themselves when they create and implement their value system.

"Establishing a value system is the first action step in creating an investment model that works toward preserving and expanding legacy.... Initial agreement on the composition and use of the values within the system is not an option; indeed it is a singular preparation to accomplishing success.

"Opportunities for success are magnified where agreed values form the cornerstone of this enterprise. An investment leader knows the importance of core values, and with the follower, creates a list of these that will be validated and ratified by both. Upon ratification, their values list provides the grid that measures the quality of their relationships (their decisions about each other's successes) and the excellence of their functions (actions that illustrate and validate those decisions). This grid becomes the standard for attitude and behavior. Shared dedication to perseverance of the standard elicits motives and desires. The system also allows that when failures come, and they will, the next exercise will be ownership, and forgiveness that is granted and received.

"The 'Twelve Laws of Understanding' ... make up a value system for the reader's consideration. A leader and follower may of course constitute their own system and form of presentation; regardless, their shared activity of creating and then ratifying such a system is one necessary step for leading and following to be effective and transferable. The more participatory involvement leader and follower share in its construction, the more opportunities for ratification and implementation the participants own.

"The 'Twelve Laws of Understanding' are laws about life and principles about living that are born out of growing understandings of fundamental truths that are as old as the rule of law for desired good.... Learn them, live them; when they are alive in you they will change lives in measurable ways, including yours, and become examples of truth enfolded into deeds—the passing of the baton, and the living of a legacy."

You are invited to read *Leadership Is—*, pages 107-114 for a full commentary on the "Twelve Laws of Understanding." These laws comprise words to live by. They are listed on the next page.

A Value System
Twelve Laws of Understanding

1. Realize I am responsible for my own choices, not others'; that changing someone else's behavior is not my responsibility; rather, I need to change me.
2. Seek to understand how the other person thinks and communicates; use his or her language.
3. Model what I want.
4. Set realistic limits on what is acceptable behavior.
5. Impose these limits on myself, first.
6. Desire the best, but prepare for difficulty; seek creative, peaceful solutions.
7. Seek and pray for wisdom.
8. Remember, at the right times.
9. Encourage always.
10. Think first, listen most, and speak seldom.
11. Realize growth involves change, change can mean pain, and patience on the journey is a virtue.
12. Love. Establish meaningful relationships.

© 2005 Glen Aubrey

Lesson 5
Leaders Are Followers First

One who leads often occupies a position with a title and benefits. Prestige, power, and authority may accompany such a place. Where leadership is driven by values and the desires to see followers succeed, positional placement fades in importance to providing opportunities for a follower's growth. In fact, leadership is all about helping followers follow well, patterning their behaviors after those of their leader.

If you are the leader, ask yourself these important questions:
1. How much do I give for the benefit of my followers?
2. How willing am I to require accountability in myself before I desire it from those I lead?
3. What are my followers learning by watching me respond to the demands fostered on me?
4. What makes a good follower?

Leaders teach followers how to follow long before they teach followers how to lead. Consider:
1. What kinds of following are your followers learning from you?
2. How have position and place given way to personal accountability and investment?
3. To what degree are you living the examples you desire to receive?

The answers to these questions are vital. You are leading well when your followers follow better because you are showing them how.

Lesson 6
Praise

Great leaders willingly offer praise to followers. They also know the importance of receiving it humbly.

Giving and receiving are parts of the same transaction, and maturing leaders know this. Exemplary leadership promotes praise as an integral part of a team's operation.

Great leaders don't falsely shun praise with an attitude of, "I really don't need affirmation." They receive it graciously as well as give it generously.

It is just as important for the leader to accept praise as it is for the follower to give it. It is just as needful for the leader to offer praise as it is for the follower to embrace it. Affirmation, when freely presented and received, is a sure indicator of genuine and strong relationships.

If you're the leader and your followers offer thanks and praise to you, take in these accolades with sincere gratitude. Followers view how you receive them and put more value on the affirmation you offer. The whole team benefits when congratulations are shared. Praise genuinely born of right motives strengthens relationships as it congratulates jobs well done.

Lesson 7
Decisions

Leaders make decisions. They have to and want to. Their processes of doing so include gathering facts, adhering to principles, and building up the people who make their decisions come to life.

Authentic decision making does not settle for surface alternatives that short-circuit right methods. Leaders understand that decisions may have long-lasting impact on people and production.

A leader's decisions tell followers what reality is. (Please read *Leadership Is An Art* by Max DePree, a book we highly recommend.) A great leader positions reality with best intent when he or she balances relationships and functions as part of decision making, emphasizing people over what they do.

Superior decision processes originate from, and must be evaluated against, the values upon which leaders and followers agree. An investing leader seeks perspectives that honor these agreed values and communicates them through decision making processes and implementation.

The decisions leaders make today determine their audiences tomorrow. Who follows you today because of prior good choices? Do followers respect you, not only because you possess and exercise decision making authority, but also because your processes consider them? What impacts on followers do you thoughtfully weigh as vital parts of making choices?

Decision making includes thoughtful consideration of the impact your decisions will have on those who follow you today. Your decisions will also influence those who become your networks tomorrow. No decision is made in isolation where followers are concerned. Who is affected by your decisions now, and who will be in the future?

Choose to lead well in your decision making. Acquire facts and consider effects. Align choices with the values that you and your followers have ratified. Better consequences will result in your people and their performance.

Lesson 8
Business Growth

When a leader decides to grow a business enterprise, positive results are not automatic. Expansion and profitability require diligent focus and hard work, sometimes way beyond what the leader originally thought was required.

If growth consequences benefit customers, vendors, and staff, then the leader decides on processes that meet the needs of these people. A leader's efforts focus on achieving best deliverables throughout the enterprise, from fulfilling the largest order to tackling the smallest but recurring internal problem.

Some leaders make the poor decision to service customers better at the expense of their staff. This combination may work for awhile but it burns out the very people that provide the improvements. This is akin to killing the goose that lays the golden egg and simply doesn't make sense.

Neither does the reverse—spending so much time on staff improvement that production and customers suffer. Then everyone goes hungry.

Build your staff so that customers are served *through* them. This makes sense and it makes dollars and cents, too. It works when open and declared agreement exists on your company's Code of Achievement: values (principles upon which you and your core team agree), vision (reasons why your organization exists), mission (tasks you accomplish and their rewards), and message (life-truths that your examples teach).

> Please see www.LeadershipIs.com to obtain *Leadership Is— How to Build Your Legacy,* where the Code of Achievement is fully explained.

Investments in your staff are seen in the quality of the goods and services they provide to your customers. If customer servicing results are not what they should be, then the problem may first rest with the leader who is not serving the staff well.

A leader understands the *a priori* need of modeling improvement to the ones who will serve the customers. A leader also realizes that a well-served and committed staff can come up with some terrific ideas for business expansion.

A leader committed to the staff, and a staff committed to serving customers based on the leader's model, form a powerful team that produces right means born of right motives. In cooperative environments like this, leaders and staff work together to grow a business. They share passion and drive. They discuss and decide what to improve, how they'll get it done, and how their customers will be better served. Business growth is the result of this cooperation.

L.E.A.D. — LEARNING, EDUCATION, ACTION, DESTINY

Ask yourself: "What do I want in growing my business? Do I desire more customers, improved service, returning sales, and stronger profits?" If so, invest in your staff first with service, reliability, and camaraderie. Let them see what you want by what you give.

Present your desires for growth and expansion to this well-served staff. Ask them for input to design programs of superior production and enhanced customer service. They will respond because they've seen it work.

The wins are multiple, of course. The wins belong to you, your teams, and customers. These groups keep your enterprise going and growing.

Remember that meeting external needs begins with investing in internal teams. People share what they have received.

Please visit **www.IndustrialStrengthSolutions.com** to purchase *Industrial Strength Solutions Build Successful Work Teams!*, the guidebook for growing effective workplace teams. Also visit **www.CoreTeamsWork.com** to order *Core Teams Work Their Principles and Practices*, and discover enhanced ways of investing in the people who make your organization work.

Lesson 9
Agreement

What values do you and your followers agree upon? How strong are these agreements? How much has your team's adherence to these agreements produced cooperation?

Agreement on the Code of Achievement (values, vision, mission, and message) is required for a leader and his or her followers who desire ongoing progress and positive tangible results. Long-lasting solutions are better obtained and firmly implemented when they come from principles upon which agreement exists.

How high is the level of team buy-in regarding what your team considers its constitution to be? How will you determine it? Begin by asking your people the questions in the first paragraph above. Chart their answers. Building agreement starts when the leader takes initiative to involve followers in a process of defining and ratifying their values, vision, mission, and message (see Lessons 2, 3, and 4).

Make areas of agreement your foundation for building stronger decisions. Positive atmospheres and exemplary task contributions emerge from these agreements.

Build on what you agree, not on what you don't. This works.

Lesson 10
Character Is Revealed When Conflict Comes

Values-driven leaders and followers communicate through the good and bad times. Their interactions include problem solving, confrontation, and the boldness to uphold right principle, no matter what.

How strong is your team when it deals with difficult issues? Do they become better through these experiences?

Conflict is not an option; indeed, it is expected. Dealing with conflict positively and providing values-based solutions to challenging issues are sure indicators of health. The opposite is also true. Dealing with conflict negatively, where isolation, demeaning criticism, intimidation, manipulation, and destructive fault finding are present, demonstrates sickness within the leader and the team.

Difficulties are simply parts of life and business experiences. They also represent opportunities for developing maturity on healthy teams. Great leaders promote positive interactions within strong relationships, where success is the product of investment, especially in dealing with tough stuff.

Conflict does not cover the essence of a vibrant relationship. Conflict reveals the strength of character the relationship produces and upon which it stands.

Lesson 11
Conflict Resolution

We agree that conflict occurs in business. It is expected, whether or not a team is healthy. It is a unifier to teams whose relationships are strong, where maturing people support each other. It is a divider where relationships are weak or absent and people tear each other down. Which describes the nature of conflict in your organization? Is conflict a builder or destroyer, and how do you know?

Stress comes in conflict. It's seen here because the raw sides of human nature are exposed in trying times. Negative circumstances are breeding grounds. Human interaction is a field where truth of character is revealed.

How does your organization handle difficulty? In confrontations, do attitudes promote dignity, self-respect, and courtesy? In disagreements are people more concerned about positive solutions than protecting turf, passing the buck, and covering up wrong doing? Your team exhibits health and is probably working well if the answers to the last two questions are yes.

When faced with conflict, if your team's environment is one where selfishness runs amuck, participants employ put-downs, intimidation stifles creativity, gossip reigns, and destructive agendas are commonplace, your team has some major fixing to do. Actions won't be repaired until the persons with the negative perspectives and practices desire changed attitudes and actions within themselves.

Core teams that want to grow in relationships and functions build positive and contributing environments where people who want to mature can do so. They don't remain in the negative and degrading ones.

Remember this: Relationship is the *decision* a team member makes about another team member's success. Function is the *action* that validates the truth of the decision. The quality of the relationship is evidenced in the behavior.

Pluses and minuses of relationships and functions are seen more in conflict than in any other place. Differing opinions, opposing agendas, procedural realignment, or error correction are stations where you and your team will surely know whether health or illness exists.

If the group isn't well, teach them to relate and function better by showing them how to make improved decisions about each other. Encourage actions born of agreed values such as mutual respect, dignity, affirmation, integrity, trust, affirmation, and open communication. Set standards to which you willingly submit, then apply these to your team's activities.

Demonstrate what you want by what you do. Ask your core team to validate the values they hold and become examples of right action toward vendors, customers, and your entire organization no matter the circumstances.

In daily commerce, conflict occurs. The question isn't if it is coming, the question is how does your team handle it when it comes?

Your organization can be exemplary. It can set standards of excellence that can be seen when trying and negative times come. Uplifting values that are not only talked about but acted upon cause a team to handle conflict better. When will your team start to treat its conflicts as opportunities for growth?

The paragraph in the text box on page 56 deals with resolving conflict. It comes from Chapter 10 of *Core Teams Work*, on page 184. Note the references from all three leadership and team development books on dealing with conflict.

Conflict resolution

Expect conflict to be a part of the human experience. Seen in work, family, social settings, or any environment where people interact, conflict is probable where more than one person is present. Because participants on a core team are not robots, they will sometimes oppose each other relationally or functionally. In fact, some of the greatest solution provision may originate from challenging interchanges. Handle them well. Conflict that divides, casts negative aspersions, builds barricades to communication, and destroys healthy relationships is generally discord that is not being dealt with appropriately or in a timely manner. If a team wants to continue to grow through trying experiences, it will find and utilize proven methods to resolve conflicts, and mature each other through the process. Open lines of communication are required, as is complete honesty and adherence to shared values. (*Leadership Is—*, pages 31, 52, 74–79, 116–118, 120, and 182; *Industrial Strength Solutions*, pages 102, 114, 137, 142, 159, 162, 193, and 209; *Core Teams Work*, pages 42–44, 90, 95, 103, 105, 111, 127, 136, 137, 165–169, 174, 177, and 178.)

Lesson 12
Frameworks

Leaders craft strong connections with followers when they make quality decisions about their follower's successes. Solid, lasting relationships are formed. Functions flourish.

Leaders do not own the successes of their followers, nor should they. Leaders fashion frameworks in which followers design and implement personal growth and group achievement. These frames are composed of the values, vision, mission, and message upon which leaders and followers agree. Remember the opening story of this book? These frameworks are the skeleton truths upon which a team organism is built.

The leader provides opportunity, definitions of wins, and procedural instruction, guiding followers as they plan and accomplish goals. Followers implement missions and fulfill requirements within frameworks constructed by the leader. These frameworks promote wholeness and excellence. Masterpieces of superior contribution emerge.

Construct lasting relationship frameworks into which your follower's functional achievements can be realized. People and their deeds will show how strong your frameworks have become.

Lesson 13
Investment

Leaders look for ways to help followers succeed. They engage in their efforts unceasingly. They invest in people who show the most promise to produce lasting and positive legacy.

Name the leaders who have impacted and influenced you. Then name those from that list who have invested in you for positive and regenerating returns. The ones on the second list most likely defined frameworks in which you learned to succeed. In the same way, investing in others is your job now if you are the leader.

The life and activities of a *willing* and *working* follower represent the greatest opportunities for the most profitable returns as you seek a follower into whom to invest. A follower's willingness and work ethic cooperate when potential for winning yields success.

If you are the leader, your leadership investments in willing and working followers benefit the entire core team. Who are the team members you are investing in?

Contributions of maturing teams outlast negative challenges that come along and demonstrate to expanding networks what great leadership is—in your life and theirs.

Lesson 14
Interaction

Leaders display strong and right relational connections through conscientious and consistent interactions with followers. These are not happenstance occurrences. Life learning seldom originates from chance encounters; rather, from changed engagements, planned and fulfilled.

Interaction that is thoughtfully conceived, initiated, and received showcases sound agreements on values, vision, mission, and message. In combination these are the foundations of actions and grids of measurement of success or failure.

Leaders design and contribute to a working and enduring model of beneficial interaction. The more consistent the leader's example is, the more lasting is the lesson it teaches. Great leaders exercise accountability, seen in consistent behaviors, demonstrating that creeds and deeds, words and works, match.

Strong relationships are firmly fixed in a team's values and connecting activities. If you are the one in charge, consider: How consistent is the alignment of principles and practices within your team's interactions? The closer the connections are to agreed values, vision, mission, and message, the more mutually beneficial these interactions will be.

Lesson 15
Relationship and Function

As a reminder, the term *relationship* is defined as the decision one makes about another team member's success. The word *function* describes the actions that prove the validity of the decision.

Relationship and function cooperate because they never can be separated. The qualities of their product are sure indicators of a team's strength and character.

Principle-based leadership proactively chooses to accomplish quality function through strengthening relationships. Positive function, therefore, is never performed isolated from its values-based relational roots. Function shows how strong and well planted the roots are.

Because people are more important than what they do, leadership builds people and intersects actions and principles. It is through relational growth that functions are completed with excellence and a team develops holistically.

It is vital that leaders continually evaluate the structures they are building as they interact with followers. Which are you building, relationships, functions, or both? Where is your primary emphasis?

You serve yourself, your company, followers, and customers best when you provision your people, investing in them relationally and functionally. The actions you see prove the quality of relationships beneath.

Lesson 16
The Storehouse of Giving

Your business thrives on profits coming from customers who pay for products or services. The more satisfied your customers are, the greater is the potential for augmented sales and commensurate profits. These fundamental business maxims are understood.

What motivates a staff member to give customers superior service and excellent products, even beyond what is expected? The answer boils down to far more than money.

Core teams produce desired and sustainable returns when they build with long-term legacy in mind. Money is simply one motivator of many, and may not be the most important one when sustainable benefits are considered.

Every business has a storehouse of giving. At one level it consists of the products and services your company provides. Your storehouse may include brick and mortar, but it is bigger than a building.

Your storehouse rests on the people of your enterprise who conduct its business functions. Your storehouse resides as much if not more in your people's attitudes and actions than in the products your customers purchase or the structure in which your people work.

Your storehouse of giving lives and contributes beyond "business as usual" when it values people as primary. Departures from mediocrity and strivings toward excellence occur when what is expected is enthusiastically exceeded because your people *desire* greatness. Enhanced effectiveness for any team doesn't originate from maintaining the status quo. It comes from people who want to grow.

Improved attitudes and actions are demonstrated on teams that return to the customer that which is first provided to them, whether monetary profits, positive attitudes, sincere appreciation, or combinations of these. Your storehouse of giving is where sharing becomes the breath of living. Giving from right motives produces returns from hearts of thanksgiving and enriches life.

Chapter 7 of *Core Teams Work* describes a "business life investment model." As noted on page 143, "Within this model, the staff comes first. Customer needs are met best when provision comes from a well-served staff. The opposite is not true. Great customer service does not automatically originate from staff personnel who are used up. Plainly stated, the customer is not, and should not be, first in priority. What the customer receives will be excellent in attitude and quality if and when the staff serving the customer is treated in these ways initially by the staff's leadership."

If you've served on a team that has been more familiar with being used up than receiving leadership's care and investment, then welcome a new opportunity to reverse this negative and destructive trend. Replace it with something superior. Your people can't give to customers what they don't already possess, so build up your people who enhance your storehouse of giving. Customers will notice, and so will you.

How improved could your customer servicing be if you first filled your staff's storehouse with the kinds of exemplary relationships and superior servicing you'd like the staff to provide to your customers? What changes would you make to see that what customers receive is a direct reflection of what your staff is given?

Invest in your staff. They will create a duplicative model of customer service that reflects the quality of service you give to them. If fact, they already are.

Expand your storehouse of giving by investing in your people as well as their products. Contribute what you want returned to the people who make your organization work.

Lesson 17
Celebrations

Leaders celebrate the successes of their followers. Celebrations come in many sizes and are made up of diverse activities. Great core teams yearn for times to honor achievement. In fact, they long for recurring and spontaneous opportunities to have a party. They love to celebrate!

Congratulate and honor the people on your team, recognizing effective decisions and noteworthy functions. Be specific and truly enthusiastic about who your people are and what they achieve. List what you and your organization accomplish that simply could not occur apart from them. These are causes for celebrations.

Genuine appreciation is never assumed. It is willfully, freely given. Because contributions come in all shapes and magnitudes, so should their corresponding celebrations. Match them. Design creative celebrations to let your people know you are thankful for their persons *and* their products.

Plan achievement-honoring events with as much dedication as you would in designing a vital business initiative. Let celebrations become a regular part of everything you and your team do. You and your team will benefit greatly.

So, when is your next party, and who will you be honoring?

Lesson 18
Seven-Step Process of Solution Provision— Dealing With Incidents and Issues

Great leaders and their core teams provide solutions to business challenges. Intricacies of methods may vary but the goals are the same—find correct answers and implement right actions to achieve desirable results.

Solution provision requires an understanding of the differences between incidents and issues. The two are not the same.

An incident is an *event*, seen in action, and the results it produces. It's a tangible occurrence placed in time and traced in activity.

An issue is a *cause* behind an incident, the reason for its occurrence. An issue is intangible and therefore may be more difficult to identify. In fact, revealing an issue may require a lot of effort.

Incidents are the *what* and issues are the *why*. Incidents may catch your team virtually unaware. Issues and their lessons can help your team prepare.

Apply the Creative Team Resources Group (CTRG) Seven-Step Process of Solution Provision. These seven action steps are sequential. The success of one builds the foundation for the next:

1. Recognize the incident.
2. Discover and deal with the issue.
3. Design solutions based on facts, causes, and desires for improvement.
4. Assign ownership of tasks and systems of reporting.
5. Perform the deeds.
6. Communicate.
7. Close the loop and evaluate success or failure.

Step 1: Recognize the incident. Know what happened. Because an incident is an event along with its accompanying effects, it should be relatively easy to see.

Most problems in day-to-day commercial activity can be described as incidents regardless of their degree of severity. Incidents reveal problems no matter their size or importance.

Step 2: Discover and deal with the issue. Know why the incident occurred. Unravel motives behind movements.

While effective leaders and teams recognize incidents, their focus doesn't remain there. Solution providers move quickly to discover roots of actions and address causes, not just symptoms. Asking why something happened is a good starting place to uncover reasons for an occurrence.

Step 3: Design solutions based on facts, causes, and desires for improvement. Once a reason is known, see and respond to the crux of the problem. Ascertain the determination of the people who want to fix the issue.

- Solution *processes* begin with *discovery* of what happened and why.
- Solution *plans* emerge from *dealing* with causes behind activity.
- Solution *provision* is revealed when people *desire* to improve their behaviors.

Facts, causes, and desires compose foundations for preferred resolutions. You need all three in this process.

Step 4: Assign ownership of tasks and systems of reporting. When Step 3 is completed, assignments follow. Listing tasks and developing systems of accountable reporting compose actions in the making.

Someone has to own behavioral changes. Identify who should assume responsibilities specifically. Write tasks down and attach a name to each. Obtain understanding and agreement from assignor and assignee of ownership of responsibility. Assure that what is desired will be performed as an action plan unfolds, that it is evaluated, corrected, or celebrated.

Design a system of reporting that considers these questions:
1. To whom will an assignee report progress?
2. How often should reports be given?
3. What form of reporting is best?

Step 5: Perform the deeds. This is where behavioral changes, verifiable actions, occur. Ideas remain ideas and "we need to..." will become "we should have..." if no one acts. When a decision and corresponding activities are decided, do them.

Performing tasks includes accomplishment with excellence, finishing well. It's more than just getting jobs done. Finishing well includes helping others achieve deliverables within higher standards. Excellence includes performance that is on time, on target, and on treasure. Excellence is not optional for dedicated core team members.

> Please see *Leadership Is—*, pages 103 and 104 for an explanation of finishing well. See *Core Teams Work*, pages 30-44 for a discussion of time, target, and treasure.

Step 6: Communicate. While communication includes sharing information, it is most effective when follow-up actions are involved. Communication is complete and learning becomes living only when behaviors change.

An assignor communicates specifics of problem resolution processes to an assignee. He or she assures that adequate and accurate information to complete the requirements is conveyed. An assignor makes a great decision about the success of an assignee when information is timely and correct, when the follower understands the role and its importance in the bigger picture, and when realistic expectations replace vacuums of unstated and therefore unrealistic outcomes.

An assignee makes a great decision about the assignor's success when he or she completes a responsibility successfully and informs the assignor of progress and closure. It's a multiple win for team members and the organization. Processes are cumulative and build upon one another. Positive results are shared.

Step 7: Close the loops and evaluate success or failure. Closing loops comprises an action and the communication of its conclusion. It requires honest evaluation conducted in an atmosphere of respect.

Closure assures that details are wrapped up and necessary information is passed along, fully understood, and responsibly owned. An effective tool to measure closure is a check list called "Communication Loop Closure: The Process of Fulfillment," found on pages 133-135 of *Core Teams Work*.

Closure blends objectives and evaluations of success or failure. The "Position Account and Contribution Evaluation" (PACE) form is an effective evaluation tool. A description of PACE is found in Chapter 6 of *Industrial Strength Solutions*, pages 113-145. The PACE form template is available on pages 219-223 of the book.

> Order *Leadership Is—How to Build Your Legacy, Industrial Strength Solutions Build Successful Work Teams!*, and *Core Teams Work Their Principles and Practices* through the CTRG online store: **www.ctrg.com**

When the sequential actions of the Seven-Step Process of Solution Provision are commenced, an incident can be framed within the context of its issue. The issue can then be addressed.

Improved actions emerge where ownership of responsibility is welcomed, communication loops are closed, and truthful and respect-generated evaluation reveals success or failure.

Incidents reveal issues. Resolving issues produces improved incidents. Or, put another way, actions emerge from motive. Improved behaviors originate from better causes.

Dealing with incidents and issues never ceases. Business demands create these challenges daily.

The Seven-Step Process of Solution Provision works no matter the number of incidents or their severity. The lessons the team learns through engaging in the process become living truths the team teaches. They are convinced these procedures work, because they've used them.

Lesson 19
A Core Team Leader's Responsibilities

Leaders willingly embrace responsibilities to help followers achieve desired results. What a leader requires *from* a follower is what the leader gives *to* the follower first.

How a leader leads is often determined by how that leader follows (see Lesson 5, page 39). Every leader is in submission to a person or entity that exercises more authority. Following comes before leading, as learning comes before educating. Great and maturing leaders continue to follow and learn well. As stated on page 18 of *Leadership Is—*, "Followers look to leaders to learn how to follow before they look to leaders to learn how to lead."

Maturing leaders choose behaviors that help them lead well. Their actions demonstrate desires for personal and core team growth and contribute mightily to success.

1. Position student and teacher, leader and follower. Establish lines of authority and accountability. These lines are essential to understanding relationships and functions.

    In order to generate success on your team, you must know who you work for and what your responsibilities are. You must understand who works with you and your obligations to them. You must appreciate who works for you and what you should contribute to them. (Please see *Leadership Is—*, pages 54-59.)

2. Promote positive relationships and contributory functions. Relational health is demonstrated in the degrees of genuine interest a leader and follower take in each other. Lip service and manipulation are not the traits of growing and vibrant relationships. Earnest listening, thoughtful responses, and motivation toward higher and realistic goals are characteristics of relational health. The leader sets the pace for what the leader wants in place.

    Activated relationships and functions build better people and products, at the same time. Communication is consistent. Cooperative problem solving is common. Investments build people up and produce strength and endurance.

3. Go where they are. Great leadership enters the environments of the people who follow. It doesn't always expect followers to come to the leader.

    While an open door policy is generally considered to be a positive attribute of a leader, drop-by leadership actively demonstrates even more authentic interest in the progress of those who are led. Engaged leaders often visit followers in their workplaces.

    Leaders who want to know go. Working environments are positively altered when a leader cares enough to come by and show genuine attention in a team member.

4. Speak their language. When leaders understand and employ the language of those they lead, they generate healthier environments. They use terms and expressions known to their followers because they are truly interested in communicating well.

   This doesn't mean that leaders dumb-down lessons or important information to audiences that may not have the leader's levels of experience, education, or environment. It does mean that leaders who educate, grasp, and understand use preferred means to communicate effectively at right times, in right places, and in right ways. When the leader genuinely wants followers to learn, stretch, and grow, the leader learns the language and the best ways of using it to assure enhanced communication.

5. Set goals. Cooperation thrives in atmospheres where people are built up and work together to define and achieve results. Here, goals are designed cooperatively.

   Silos and stovepipes are diminished or removed. Allowed to exist, they would prevent synergetic goal setting. Communication blockades are characteristics of negative and claustrophobic environments, so an effective leader identifies and gets rid of them, replacing them with structures that promote energetic exchange and symbiotic relationships.

   Goal setting in contributory atmospheres considers multiple opportunities, determines viable options, decides processes, plans well, and aligns right people

with action steps.
6. Chart progress. Big wins are important, but so are the incremental steps that help a core team achieve grand prizes. Charting progress of large and small contributions is a healthy exercise.

    Observing achievement includes evaluating how valuable resources, including people, are utilized and replenished. Success stories chronicle noteworthy advances. A leader is informed of successes of his or her team in order to recognize and celebrate great returns on investments of time, target, and treasure. (Please see "Chapter 9: You Can Bank on It," beginning on page 172 of *Core Teams Work*.)
7. Evaluate success and failure. Evaluation is not optional if a leader and core team want to assess wins and losses. Avoidance of evaluation for fear of upsetting a boss or employee demonstrates a leadership vacuum and disconnect within the team.

    Evaluation procedures reveal the core traits of the people on the team. When assessments are performed in relationally strong environments, evaluations are characterized by attitudes of openness, willingness to share praise, genuine congratulations, and profound truth telling. Great evaluations refuse intimidation, short-sightedness, argumentative discussions, condescension, or other behaviors of insufficient and inadequate communication.
8. Celebrate wins and affirm one another. Honoring

achievement is as important as evaluating process, perhaps even more so. How often does your team celebrate?

Leaders who value people over production extol their team members, their progress and productivity, from hearts of genuine thanks and affirmation.

Methods of core team leadership demonstrate commitments to followers and their success. How does your core team leadership measure up?

Lesson 20
Close the Loops

Leaders enjoy seeing communication loops closed, especially when followers wrap up loose ends because they've learned how to do it from the leader's instruction and example. Communication loops are closed when deeds are done with excellence and results are communicated to the people who need to know.

Leadership establishes, exercises, and reinforces positive behaviors in front of followers. Resolving problems and closing loops are common experiences that show followers how leaders learn, educate, and act.

Leaders teach how to close the loops. They know instructions are required, should continually be reviewed, and must be consistently reinforced. Closure processes must never be assumed. Time spent educating these techniques is valuable and remains a high priority (please see *Core Teams Work*, pages 133-135 for instructions on completing tasks and closing the loops).

Healthy teams endeavor to learn and practice closure processes consistently. What are some of the methods you and your core team employ in closing the loops and how often do you teach them?

Lesson 21
Thankfulness

Thankful is an old-fashioned term. Unfortunately, its application is not utilized nearly enough in postmodern business. According to Merriam-Webster's 11th Collegiate Dictionary, the meaning of the adjective *thankful* includes "conscious of benefit received" and "expressive of thanks." *Thankfulness*, the noun, is the corresponding attitude and action of a truly grateful person or group. Thankfulness is an obvious characteristic of health.

Great core teams are composed of thankful people. Acts of giving and receiving are integral parts of what they do.

Grateful people understand the value and validity of being thankful, and of giving and receiving praise. Involved and caring team members know how to offer praise when they genuinely and gratefully accept it.

If you are following a good leader, affirm him or her. If you are the leader, receive your followers' praise. Appreciate your team and let them know by thanking them. Learn the art of mutual giving and receiving.

Thankfulness is a mark of health and maturity. Leader and followers are always better for the interchange.

Lesson 22
Success Through Mentoring

A leader is happy when a follower matures, particularly when results are related to the leader's investment in the follower. Everyone loves this kind of success.

At Creative Team Resources Group, Inc., we define success as "seeing another person realize their dreams and goals through encouragement and support." (This definition is located in *Leadership Is—*, on page 9).

Which of your followers are producing positive results you can readily observe? Which of your people appear to struggle or to not want to move from where they are now? What is your reaction when you see a follower with potential not maximizing efforts to achieve more?

Mentoring is a preferred method a leader chooses to help a follower succeed. The leader's role is to clearly define the goals of a mentoring investment with the follower. The follower's responsibility is to learn from the leader and apply truth in life. Both leader and follower determine if they are ready for such an engagement.

A well-placed mentoring investment is worth the time, energy, and resources it requires. Mentoring includes mutual agreement of purpose, goals, actions, timelines, responsibilities, and reporting so that resources are maximized and utilized well. (Please see *Leadership Is—,* pages 130-135, where the process of mentoring is explained.)

Resources are best utilized when leader and follower willfully agree on their mentoring goals and procedures. Holistic growth and maturity, as well as development of skills and capabilities, can be the welcomed results of a mentoring investment focused on success.

Lesson 23
Nurture and Support

Leaders engage in acts of nurture and support on behalf of their followers. Nurture and support are integrated parts of a balanced mentoring process. They produce beneficial traits and qualitative results. So let's define these terms.

Nurture is help offered from the *outside in*, where the viewpoints of the leader originate from an objective and caring position. Nurture sees what is needed for improvement and speaks truth in atmospheres of relational warmth. Nurture originates from a leader's decision to promote a follower's success, even if the process is uncomfortable. The purpose of nurturing is to present truth, to help a follower work through difficulty. Where a relationship is strong, nurture is possible and likely won't include the defense postures that accompany truth telling in weak relationships.

Support is assistance offered from the *inside out*, where empathy, understanding, and binding form a base of encouragement and celebration. Support is need identification and encouragement at soul-touching levels. It is usually warmly received if not requested. Support is easier to give (and receive) simply because it feels better.

A balanced leader-follower relationship accepts and exercises both nurture and support. In fact, these two actions are common. Who is receiving this balanced investment from you? (Please see *Leadership Is—*, pages 165-168, where the descriptions and applications of nurture and support are discussed.)

Lesson 24
Engaged Leadership—The Process of Connecting

Pro-action replaces reaction when leadership is appropriately engaged. Circumstances may take a detached leader by surprise. But involved leadership, anchored on values, vision, mission, and message, sees challenges as possibilities for growth, seizes moments of change as opportunities for development, and implements strong solutions. This leadership is prepared because it is connected.

What kinds of leadership do you exercise with your core team? Attached leadership begins with a commitment to connect with the people who follow you. Involved leaders are not isolated, even though they may require solitude on occasion. Attached leadership purposefully strengthens relationships, whether in pleasant or difficult circumstances. How well connected are you with your followers?

Leadership Is— (pages 57-59) presents four questions a leader asks a follower to encourage connection. Leaders propose these questions to engage followers because they understand the mutual benefits the connection provides.

The Four Questions are:
1. Who are you at your core? (A question of values)

2. What is your life's passion, calling, or cause? (A question of vision)
3. What do you want? (A question of mission)
4. Whom will you impact? (A question of message)

An engaged and proactive leader is not removed from followers who want to mature. Leadership connections prepare followers for work's inevitable changes. Connectivity generates frameworks in which success is achievable.

If developing attached leadership is your goal, then move closer to your followers. See what the proximity reveals. It is in closer association that a leader and follower demonstrate desires to mature through mentoring. Here the leader and follower possess golden opportunities for teaching and modeling the behaviors they both want.

L.E.A.D. — LEARNING, EDUCATION, ACTION, DESTINY

Lesson 25
Creating Workplace Positives

Attitudes and actions are choices. This isn't news, of course. But what may be news is the degree that positive attitudes and actions contribute to uplifting work environments—for the one who serves and the one who's served.

Try this test: Smile. Practice it again in front of a mirror. Now find a workplace partner and smile at him or her with sincerity and joy.

If you thought you were going to be asked for the reaction from the person who saw you smile, you're not. Instead, how did *you* feel when you did it?

Have you ever driven into a parking lot where an attendant was working? This person's purpose is to assign you a place, issue a time stamped ticket, and take your money. When is the last time that a parking lot attendant smiled and waved at you because he or she was genuinely glad for your business? Would smiling make a positive difference to you or the attendant? It probably would, if it made you both feel more welcome and appreciated.

Positive outcomes are often generated from the smallest of efforts: smiling, waving, exchanging thoughtful greetings (not perfunctory ones), where attention is clearly focused on raising the prospects for the one on the receiving end. And that is the key. The right motive is what is given, not what is expected in return.

We've learned that giving and receiving are parts of the same action. Motives and choices encourage ones who desire more satisfying and uplifting work environments to take initiative to infuse positives into another's experience.

Think of giving as an investment. Dividends from contributing positive attitudes and actions grow exponential returns, and it doesn't take long to see them.

Instigate workplace positives. Start with the small ones. Turn to someone on your core team, genuinely smile, and wish them a good day. Make eye contact. Focus on them because you want to give them a gift. Don't wait for the return. It will come. In fact, the return may be seen when the person who received your gift presents positive treatment to others on the job site.

Positive attitudes and actions are contagious. Use them without reservation.

Lesson 26
Recognizing and Pursuing Personal Opportunity

Does opportunity knock or do you have to reach for it? Well, yes.

Twenty-first century high-speed business connectivity provides limitless opportunities for learning. Methods to acquire knowledge, achieve position, grow responsibility, and earn commensurate wealth are endless.

Opportunities are easy to discover but they may be harder to maximize because there are so many of them. Opportunities outnumber viable options.

When should an opportunity become a worthwhile objective and how can you know? Here are perspectives and calls to action that may help:

1. Start with your dreams—what are they? Turn dreams into desires. Describe what you really want. Understand your passions on the basis of who you are and what you believe you can contribute. Best success options shouldn't contradict inward character or innate gifts.
2. Set your goals. These are time-sensitive mile-markers, specific activities against which success or failure must

be measured.

    Whether you recognize opportunity or have to create it, take the initiative. If you truly desire best processes and superior end deliverables for yourself and those you care about, then get moving. Don't give up and don't cave in.

3. "If you want to shoot a moose, go to where the moose are." In other words, if there is a field of opportunity that interests you, seek information and realistic options there. Interview people who are practicing in your field of interest. Ask about their celebrations, challenges, and choices. Explore. Venture.
4. Analyze costs and risks. Weigh these against projected benefits. What will your efforts require in time, energy, and money to turn an opportunity into a profitable option? What are the risks? How willing are you to take them? What are the projected benefits of success? How willing are you, or should you be, to venture beyond what you know toward expanded horizons that cause you to grow?
5. Learn the difference between capability and call. Capability is made up of what you *can* do. Call is composed of what you *should* do.

    Contributions in any environment represent both capability and call in varying degrees. Which deserves the majority of your effort?

    Most people possess a long list of capabilities. These actions are well within their scopes of success. But spending too much time on them may be a detractor from superior choices of living and contributing within call and passion.

Actions based on call are fulfilling to you and your networks. The effects are far reaching.

Where are you mainly living and working—in capability or call? How much of your contributory time exists in what you are *able* to do as opposed to what you're *supposed* to do?

Evaluate opportunities and options against what you believe your call or passion to be. What do you discover? What portions of your call match your viable options? How close are you to start fulfilling them now?

Seek opportunities, seize them, sift and evaluate them. Listen to wise counsel, choose best alternatives, pursue diligently, and fulfill your call no matter your vocation. *In fact, starting to fulfill a call may begin right where you work and improve what you are already doing.* Life is too short to dwell beneath your potential.

Recognizing and pursuing opportunity is much more than reviewing your To Do items on tomorrow's list. The quest requires diligence and dedication. It may demand hard sacrifices of time, energy, and other valuable resources. It will command your utmost attention to excellence regardless of circumstances.

The journey is the destination. The means are more important than the ends. Your journey of personal opportunity begins the moment you recognize it exists.

L.E.A.D. — LEARNING, EDUCATION, ACTION, DESTINY

Lesson 27
Integrity

Leadership that builds positive and contributing legacies is grounded on enduring principles of truth, right standing, honesty, and faithfulness. Together, these form integrity.

A company line, if it includes a need to compromise integrity, shall not influence the leader who is unalterably committed to far more than surface convenience. If an action to meet the need of the moment violates integrity, that action will not be considered.

Integrity is a way of thinking and acting. A person of integrity doesn't degrade the means to justify the ends. He or she practices methods that uphold enduring and endearing principles no matter the costs. Great leaders exercise integrity as the rule, not the exception. These leaders expect the same behavior from dedicated followers.

Leaders of integrity tell the truth in spite of difficulty, risks, or embarrassment. They set high standards of people investment when they do. Longevity and resilience, seen in reliable character, take center stage for the person committed to leading well for the right reasons and in the right ways.

To what degree, if any, are you willing to sacrifice your character to fulfill perceived or real changes or chances? Hopefully the answer is none.

Costs of vacuums of integrity are monumental. They abide in the remains of deceitful endeavors and live in the remembrances of those affected by poor decisions born of impure and dishonorable motives.

Lesson 28
Great People and Great Production

Great leaders invest in committed individuals to achieve best deliverables. Results are seen in maturing people and heightened output. Investments into committed followers outlast the leader and produce exponential rewards over time.

Conversely, poor leaders shun investment, choosing domination and control. Ineffective leaders push people to become something they are not, or manipulate them to produce what they otherwise should not. They are not, in any stretch of imagination, exercising what great leaders practice.

Investing in people is the central goal of the dedicated leader. That leader knows that two results are achieved. Benefits may occur simultaneously or sequentially. These positive outcomes are:
1. Great People
2. Great Production

An investment that produces only one of these is not complete.

Where people are valued merely on the basis of what they produce investment leadership is absent. When people are valued on personal worth as well as what they produce, balanced leadership is working.

It is refreshing when a workplace provides a growth space for people as well as their contributions, recognizing and honoring the journeys and benefits of both. In healthy organizations, this is common.

Which characterizes your work environments: people who are developing and are inspired by leadership, or people who are valued for just what they produce? How much leadership in your organization composes a contact that encourages growth versus a contract that inhibits it?

How would you change a negative function-driven culture to a responsible relationship-driven one, where improved decisions about people's success permeate atmospheres and beget superior functions? One way: Treat people and yourself from a relationship-driven and function-inclusive mindset because people are more important than what they do. Convince yourself of this unalterable truth. Then tell them you believe it about yourself and about them. Prove you mean it. Your environment will improve.

Production is necessary. It's one of the main reasons business exists. No argument there. But great leaders understand functional as well as relational duties. These leaders build business production *through* their people, not in spite of them. These leaders build positive legacies in the lives and contributions of their followers.

Lesson 29
Rewarding Achievement

Leaders honor and congratulate followers for their victories. Celebrations are important to the core team's life.

Completing one project and immediately moving on to the next without recognition, thanksgiving, or praise is not appropriate. In fact, it's wrong. A vacuum of recognition is demoralizing. It tells the producers they are only as valuable as their completed project.

Expenditures of time, resources, and energy are required to honor success. Be prepared to spend them. Reward and thank the people who work hard for you and your enterprise. Establish a budget for this investment. *In tough times, this is the last budget item that should be touched.* (Read that sentence again.)

Was there a time when you accomplished a goal for which you were not recognized or thanked? Compare this to one when you were genuinely rewarded and praised for your achievement. Which motivated you more?

Far more than good feelings are in play here. Dignity of person and credit for performance are combined when appreciation is sincere and exercised often. From *Leadership Is—*, page 97: "Leaders know the value of wins and congratulate progress in various ways throughout the process. Leaders who build legacies comprehend worth of ongoing recognition. Leader and follower understand, because it has been communicated many times and in many ways that leadership is constantly looking for a follower's daily cause to celebrate, regardless of size.

"Leaders itch for a triumph, are 'on the watch' to catch their people in the act of doing things well and notice them, right then! ...Causes for celebration are observed quicker when relationships are strong and communication procedures active. If you as the leader haven't seen many successes in your follower lately, how much of the cause of this oversight comes from a lack of relational connectivity?"

A leader chooses rewards that recognize achievement. Choices are as varied as the individuals who receive them. One sure way to hit the mark is to ask how people like to be recognized and affirmed. Their answers are telling, so pay attention. Three categories usually emerge:
1. Verbal praise
2. Written appreciation
3. Objects of value (money, gifts)

Rewards are freely given out of respect and in recognition of fulfilled goals and faithful service. Not all accomplishments are the same so reward systems don't have to be identical, either. Tailor recognitions to the person and their accomplishments as you would assign the right person to an appropriate task.

Lesson 30
Interdependence

Leaders have their followers' best interests at heart when they fashion working relationships of interdependence. Operating in this environment is a worthy goal. The good news is that it is achievable.

Most leader-follower relationships begin in a state of dependence. Here a follower leans heavily on the presence and personality of the leader. This leadership state is categorized as *impact* leadership.

A stronger leader-follower relationship is formed when the leader exercises positional authority over, and responsibility for, the follower's actions. This is a state of *influence*. It is common in postmodern business cultures. It is noted for reliance on policies, procedures, authoritative structures, and job requirements. Here seeds of independence may be planted and start to sprout. A follower who wants to grow will exhibit desires to mature and develop self-sufficiency.

A higher level of the leader-follower relationship is one of interdependence, where establishing and guaranteeing legacy occurs. This is a state of *investment*. Strengthened and long-lasting conditions of interaction are practiced. Leader and follower work together, nurturing and supporting each other. In this state, the follower is taught by the leader how to fulfill goals and produce more than the leader, accomplishing greater works. Superior leadership and engaged following thrive here. This is where leaders apprentice followers for mutual and duplicative returns.

If you are the leader consider these questions: How much do your followers depend on you? To what degree do they want to advance into relationships of independence? Who are the up and coming followers, those with passions for excellence and desires to grow? With whom do you share working relationships of interdependence where you and those you lead mature and contribute to each other's success?

> For more information on leadership impact, influence, and investment, read *Leadership Is—*, Chapter 2.

Lesson 31
The Essence of Great Leadership

Leadership is more than a concept, calling, or inherent gift. While it may include these attributes, at its core it's a choice. Therefore, achieving great leadership is reachable to people who desire to help others succeed.

A great leader cares more about the follower's growth than the leader's title or position. This leader considers people as valuable because they are people, not in just what they contribute to an enterprise. Many who are in positions of power and authority may be leading, but are not leading well if their outlooks and treatments of people recognize work alone and shun honoring personal worth.

Analyze your work environment. How do you treat your people? How do other leaders and coworkers treat them? Does leadership in your work place build those who follow, or use them up? If you are the leader, how do you view your followers?

People are more important than what they do. This rock solid truth is the foundation for leadership that lives and constructs enduring and uplifting legacies.

Leadership that reaches beyond comfort and complacency abhors mediocrity in relationships and functions. This leadership cares about people and what they produce. It helps team members mature in decisions and tasks.

Enduring leadership invests. The assignment is not easy to fulfill. It requires work, effort, money, time, and firm dedication. Is it worth it?

Durable results of great leadership investments are these:
1. Followers grow in cooperation with the leader's example, not in spite of it.
2. Leaders and followers practice open communication.
3. Leaders and followers agree on principles of integrity, employ a strong work ethic, showcase faithfulness to duty, and complete tasks with excellence.
4. Leaders empower followers to become better than their leaders.
5. Improved products and services result.
6. A stronger bottom line is a by-product.
7. Reliability and accountability are enhanced.

When genuine interest is taken in people and production, solutions to common and uncommon problems become doable. In fact, thinking and acting from a solution-driven perspective become rules, not exceptions.

If you are the leader and want to create positive, uplifting, and productive work environments, make the decision to invest in your followers. If you are a follower, make your work situation better.

L.E.A.D. — LEARNING, EDUCATION, ACTION, DESTINY

Model the behaviors you desire your leader to exercise. Decisions about another person's success go both ways.

Please visit **www.IndustrialStrengthSolutions.com** to order *Industrial Strength Solutions,* the guidebook for workplace solution thinking and action.

L.E.A.D. — LEARNING, EDUCATION, ACTION, DESTINY

Lesson 32
Change Is Challenging

Even for those who say they embrace and enjoy it, change can be a challenge. The leader who promotes best people, practices, and production understands healthy and required change, preparing and assisting followers to go through it and learn from it.

Changing behavior for improved outcomes is a mark of maturity. Better actions should accompany fresh and beneficial information.

Leaders react to news, prepare for it, and sometimes create it. Leaders anticipate change. They plan for the future. They help followers understand why positive behavior alteration is required as a part of growing up.

How does your team handle change? Who are the positive change agents on the team? If you are the leader, consider this: How often do you initiate needful change and prepare your people for it, giving them solid reasons and walking them through processes of growth?

What changes are coming for you? What changes are coming from you? How should they be handled for the good of your team and your organization?

Ways to handle change are varied, of course. They are understood better and performed best when behaviors align with ratified values, vision, mission, and message, the Code of Achievement (see page 29). Changes can be faced with surety and confidence when your people are secure in this code. Without it, change can be daunting and encourage doubt.

Maturing people grow through change processes. They become stronger for the experiences when anchored on principles that do not shift.

Lesson 33
A Fresh Perspective

"Let's look at this differently, with a fresh perspective, an alternate mind-set."
"Should we consider other options?"
"What are newer ways of tackling this problem?"
"I read about a fresh approach. May I tell you about it?"
"Let's come up with something better."
"What about this idea?"

New views are afforded opportunity to become true views when a team decides to observe them from varied perspectives. When was the last time you and your team considered circumstances and actions from more than one viewpoint?

Business moves quickly. Within commerce speed is king and small is queen. Providing sufficient time and space to regard opportunities from differing perspectives is too often sacrificed on an altar of expediency, and that's dangerously high risk.

Some decisions, usually the big ones, require deeper contemplation and more consideration than business timelines may want to allow. Hasty decisions birth wasteful results, however, when decisions to act are not born from carefully weighed ideas and facts.

Observing and considering new views mean, first of all, that facts have to be accumulated—probably from many sources—then evaluated carefully. A wise business person asks questions of people who are positioned with good information in order to be assured that the information is as front line accurate as possible. Obtaining facts from a single source may not, and usually is not, the best course. Without necessary facts, decisions can be inopportune or completely wrong.

Adopting an attitude of openness to alternative views is a hallmark of the growing leader and core team. How often do you invite open discussion in an atmosphere of positive reinforcement because you want to encourage your people to make a difference?

"What do you think?" is a great question to get perspective discussions going. A good follow up question is "why?" Pose this simple question with sincerity, from a genuine desire to learn.

Requesting and receiving diverse opinions shows confidence in your leadership and your people. As your business develops, you will continually face fresh opportunities and challenges. How much do you desire to confront them with more than the redundant "We've always done it this way" answers?

Admonish members to discover and investigate varying perspectives. Encourage them to seize and weigh new opportunities. Ask them to design action steps for follow through and evaluation.

Your people may come up with unbelievably good solutions to business challenges. But you must provide the time and space to encourage creative perspectives to be shared.

It takes a strong leader to do this. How strong are you in this regard?

Lesson 34
Reflections

Mirrors are reflective surfaces. So are core teams. Working groups reflect the character and perspectives of the leader whom they serve, especially when times are tough.

If you are the leader, what do the activities of your core team say about you? Clearly, team members own individual responsibility for their choices of behavior. But the leader bears tremendous accountability along with accompanying authority.

Consider negative attitudes and activities originating from an unhealthy team. Should a leader be answerable for a group's dysfunction?

The broad answer, in a word, is yes. And here's why: Regardless of the state of health or dysfunction of the team, the leader is the one who must imbue the group with values that promote positive behaviors and confront negative ones. Destructive attitudes and actions should not be tolerated—they should be fixed. A leader constructs frameworks to help a team correct dysfunction because that is part of the leader's role. These frameworks are made up of the team's values, vision, mission, and message.

Great leadership allocates necessary time to encourage and educate core team members to produce desired outcomes, promoting good ones and diminishing bad ones. Among the tasks a maturing leader accomplishes are these:

1. Assess current conditions of relationships and functions.
2. Create atmospheres that promote welcomed behaviors, tied to agreed values.
3. Teach team members what improved behavior is.
4. Declare values-driven expectations of conduct.
5. Model preferred behaviors. The leader shows what he or she wants *from* the team by demonstrating these behaviors *to* them initially.
6. Provide stability and accountability.
7. Promote solution thinking and acting.
8. Evaluate procedures on a recurring basis.
9. Correct errors.
10. Celebrate results.
11. Reward competence.
12. Do these steps all over again.

Great teams look and act like their leader. So do dysfunctional ones. Teams model what they learn from the top.

Leadership and core team effectiveness is not accidental. It is intentional, motivated by people growth, inclusive of results, and inspired by leadership.

Initiatives for growth and perseverance toward greatness begin with leadership. If the one in charge discharges duties faithfully, positive results should be expected. If you are the leader, ask yourself:

1. What does the image my team portrays say about my leadership effectiveness?
2. How do our profit margins show my dedication to responsible stewardship of resources, including money?
3. How beneficial is my leadership to my core team?
4. What actions can I take to improve my leadership and when will I start?

A team reflects its leader's characteristics as a mirror reveals an image. The leader creates the truthful portrayal of relationships and functions that should compose a great core team. A growing leader improves his or her behaviors, then teaches and models them through words and deeds that match. This reflection is not distorted, scratched or marred. This reflection is accurate—a portrayal of what is and of what is desired.

Lesson 35
Goals

Goals are necessary—we know this. Breaking them into doable pieces, constructing timelines in which they are accomplished, and consistently evaluating and reporting success or failure are processes of goal fulfillment.

Leaders change the perception that agreed goals and due dates can be ignored or forgotten. A leader identifies worthwhile objectives with his or her teams. This leader solicits and may require participation so that the people with the ideas may become the implementors once goals and actions are decided.

Leaders ask the team to break out overall objectives into time managed work plans to assure movement. Calendar sensitive work plans are not optional if a goal is to be fulfilled on time, with excellence, communication, and closure.

Leaders help teams track progress. Leadership is working well when the team reports status back to the leader because they want to and the leader doesn't have to chase down information or hound people to do their jobs.

Establishing goals with a core team is more than talking about them.

1. It requires transferring ownership of tasks to the people who get the jobs done.
2. It means agreeing on priorities of task accomplishment, establishing timelines, and assigning people for fulfillment.
3. It includes supplying needed resources and tools. Without them, goals fall into the category of unrealistic expectations and ultimately expire.

Faithful people, stewards of tasks, timelines, targets, and treasures receive great satisfaction from accomplishing agreed goals. Leaders celebrate them and their successes.

Setting goals, achieving them, recognizing achievement, and rewarding results are marks of improving and growing leadership. How well does your team's goal fulfillment measure up?

Lesson 36
Restoring Relationships on a Team

Leaders author processes of resolution and reconciliation. When parties who labor together are not working well, the leader who cares becomes the leader who gets involved, bringing opposing people together.

While functional problem resolution is the goal, it may be next to impossible to fully achieve without initial relationship reconciliation. The process may not be easy. Indeed, it can be difficult, consuming valuable time and energy. But where firm desires exist for parties to come together to build synergistic union, the costs may be worth it.

The leader's responsibilities are to:
1. Recognize incidents.
2. Identify issues.
3. Clarify where relationships are broken.
4. Bring opposing parties together to solve difficulties.
5. Verify that relationship reconciliation and functional resolution is desired.
6. Work to achieve improved behaviors.
7. Encourage if not require altered and improved behaviors. Rebuilding relationships and functions never occurs apart from changing behaviors.

The order of these actions is important. Designing and implementing systems of restoration includes putting working relationships back together before resolving the functional problems the relational disconnect has caused. These efforts begin with values agreement. It is here that desires for something better are produced. No actions of rebuilding relationships endure beyond an emotional moment unless solid agreement on values is obtained. Solving functional disconnect becomes a real possibility, however, when that agreement exists.

If you are the leader who is consistently called upon to solve problems (especially recurring ones with the same people), who enters the ring way too often to separate combatants or regularly acts as judge and jury over repetitious thorny problems, then you may wish to look deeper to discover where responsible reconciliation and resolution should occur. You will work to establish desired results upon which parties can and should agree (see Lesson 18, page 71).

Bring people together on the basis of agreement. Build foundations of reconciliation and resolution that outlast dysfunction and require better behaviors.

Lesson 37
Emerging Leadership, Building People—It's Not New

Too often leadership is viewed as acquired power, position, title, and tenure. Leaders whose primary or sole objective is to produce according to product- and profit-driven motives may manipulate and push their followers, strengthening their bottom line at all costs. They may manage working personnel from a utilitarian perspective where team members are valued only because of what they produce.

A refreshing system of leadership thinking and acting is emerging. In fact, it is taking the work world by storm. And it should. Leadership models that push production over people are fading because they must. Their character is faulty at the core. The mechanical and manipulative means-to-an-end methods of doing business are dying natural deaths because they should.

The alternate system places people as more important than production. It changes ways of living, working, leadership, and following. It endures beyond the moment and lives within its destiny.

But this new system of thinking and acting is really not new at all. In fact it's been around for a very long time. Leaders and teams are simply rediscovering and applying it.

Formerly described as the "soft underbelly side of business," or as "soft skills," the relationship-first and function-second paradigm is again proving its worth because it is superior. And it is not soft. A decision to build people is one of the most difficult, though worthwhile, choices a great leader and willing follower make and implement. The decision costs time, energy, and resources. It requires sacrifice and dedication. Here the leader is placed in a position of accountability *to* followers before requiring proofs *from* them. The follower is positioned to give the leader a great return on investment in personal growth and functional excellence. This is hard work, but right.

Legacy-driven leaders pave paths for followers to win. They help them achieve goals that contribute to success. In fact, a great leader succeeds when he or she sees another person achieve his or her dreams, often contributing tools, time, training, and talent to promote the follower's win.

If you are the leader, what standards or systems of leadership do you employ? Are they founded on power, position, tenure, or title? Or do they include giving, sacrifice, great decisions about follower's successes, and support regardless of costs?

Make better decisions about your leadership. Build frameworks where your people discover their talents, gifts, abilities, competencies, and the pathways to realize their dreams. Invest in them and grow something that will outlast you.

This is no theoretical concept that needs contemporary validation. Proof of its endurance arises whenever leadership is born of values, vision, mission, and message.

If you and your group want enduring leadership and exemplary improvements within people and production, then activate this old, new leadership with them. Simply put, it works.

Lesson 38
It's All About Details

Little things matter—a lot.

Going through an airplane parts manufacturing facility, I was struck at the myriad of devices that are installed in a wing. All are required for that vital accessory to function. Management of inventory is computer-controlled, but human interface remains important. Humans check and recheck assemblies to assure quality and inclusion of vital elements.

For example, take an O-ring. The one I viewed was about the size of a quarter. When it is correctly placed and operational, a wing hydraulics assembly is complete. Without the O-ring functioning properly, leaking occurs and the hydraulics of the wing could fail. That little ring is important! It is checked to guarantee that it is manufactured to exacting specifications and is installed correctly. Working without fail is not optional.

In every business there are O-rings that leaders and managers must be aware of. They represent the small details often referred to as minutiae. But success or failure of bigger agendas may rest squarely upon them.

One challenge for leaders is to keep the big picture in focus without micromanaging tinier aspects of its execution. Each member on a core team should own specific responsibilities and attend to details. Each member should assure their portion of the "wing" is operational.

Followers look to leaders to learn how to handle the details. Leaders who are thorough in their own follow-through set an example of pace and faithfulness. They demonstrate balance between seeing a project holistically and fulfilling specifics no matter how small and unobserved these may be.

How much does your team count on you to follow through on your tasks? How can they be convinced you will handle the small details you need to accomplish?

It should never be assumed that smaller details will be automatically handled. The proof they are dealt with lies in doing the deeds and reporting them done. Here's the rule: The one who wraps up smaller duties assures those to whom he or she reports that these tasks are fully completed. Their execution and accountable reporting allow bigger agendas to flourish and be faithfully performed.

Consider the O-rings of your operation. How are they being done? Who owns responsibilities of handling the small tasks?

Here's a check list of action points that may help you and your team to better attend to details:
    1. Who owns the management of a project or a portion of it?

2. What is the timeline for completion?
3. What are our reporting systems and to whom?
4. Who faithfully attends to the details?
5. How important is double checking and who owns this responsibility?
6. If details are seen as perfunctory or not needful what kind of damage could this conclusion cause?
7. How often do we check our systems to assure needs of production, regardless of size, are adequately met?
8. What improvements in systems management are justified, when will we make them, and who owns this improvement?

The leader and team who attend to the O-ring details rightly feel comfortable as a project, or their portions of it, comes to completion.

1. The members of the team count on each other.
2. They manage the specifics of their operations well.
3. They contribute to the success of others who depend on their commitments to excellence.

The O-rings are important. Make sure your core team knows this and gets the details done.

Lesson 39
Leaders Communicate

Effective leaders model the kinds of communication they desire. They want accurate information to be given and received. They want verification that what was said was what was heard.

You've heard the expression "lost in transmission." That condition, unfortunately, happens too often in work group communication.

How does a leader assure that what has been said is what has been heard? One of the best ways is to ask open-ended questions of the listener (open-ended questions are those that cannot be answered with a yes or no) or request feedback to assure understanding. This interchange could include comments or questions like, "Please repeat back what you heard me say—I want to be sure I was clear," "What are you taking away from this discussion?" "What are your action steps?" and "What points resonate with you?"

The same rule applies when a leader listens. The leader should offer to state back what has been said to verify accuracy and comprehension.

Respectful, clear, and receptive communication techniques reveal desires of those who make decisions about another's success.

If one really wants to communicate, that person strives to hear and speak well.

Say it right, hear it right, and repeat it right to assure transmission is error-free.

> For more information on communication methods, please review Chapter 6 of *Core Teams Work*, "Team Communication—Examples that Endure," beginning on page 124.

Lesson 40
It's About Time

Timing is everything. We've heard it before. But let's state it a different way: Let's conclude that time utilization is everything.

Whenever I hear someone say "I don't have time," I interpret their comments to mean they don't have sufficient interest, the proposition under consideration is not their priority, or they are simply refusing to engage.

All of us have the same amount of time. How we use it is where priorities become known.

Ignoring reporting requirements, overlooking assignments, and fulfilling jobs late are indicators of lack of self-discipline and lax time management. When "I don't have time" permeates a working environment you can count on customer's needs not being met, communication loops not being closed, and expectations not being realized.

Organizing time is a worthwhile objective. So, how to do it? At CTRG, we teach the value of establishing and calendaring action steps for virtually every interaction. If we conduct a meeting and don't walk away with action steps, specifically placed on a calendar to which participants are committed, then we have wasted our energy and time as well as someone's money, probably our own.

At the conclusion of your next meeting, avoid leaving discussed actions "dangling." A sure sign of time sensitive follow-through is when team members desire to be part of an action, commit to doing their jobs, and establish time lines of activity and reporting. A sign of non-committal is when a team does not write actions down, is not specific regarding due dates, does not assign or accept responsibilities for completion and reporting, and simply lets time and responsibility flitter by.

What kind of "it's about time" organization do you have? Is time your ally or an excuse used too often to avoid commitment?

When time is a partner, dedication to proper and profitable utilization will soar. So will your results: more satisfied customers, greater profits, increased returning sales, and a staff that can congratulate itself on jobs well done.

Time is one of three essentials for success described in Chapter 1 of *Core Teams Work*. This chapter, titled "On Time, on Target, on Treasure," treats time as a precious resource, one that should never be wasted. Using time wisely honors people and their processes. Wasting time violates the principle of a strong work ethic and shows little desire for another's success.

Ask your core team and yourself:
    1. How do we value our work time?

2. What are the indicators we are using time well?
3. What are evidences that we are not utilizing time as well as we should?
4. What specific and immediate change actions would contribute to more efficient use of work time?
5. How dedicated are we to concluding meetings where right and verifiable actions are assigned within specific time frames?
6. What kinds of long-range improvements should we expect when time is used more efficiently?
7. What behavioral changes will I make to assure better utilization of time, when will I make these changes known, and to whom?

Where time is treated as a resource to be invested, commitments follow that assure returns from its expenditure. It is not wasted.

Time once used is gone. Remind your team often how important time is and to use it well.

L.E.A.D. — LEARNING, EDUCATION, ACTION, DESTINY

Lesson 41
Planning

Planning is necessary. We know this. It's common sense. Unfortunately its practice isn't common enough. When activities, processes, or products don't achieve desired levels of excellence, it may well be because someone didn't plan purposely enough or set success parameters in place.

Planning begins when project ideas become goals born of concept or directive. So if product XYZ is our deliverable, how do we achieve it?

Planning is more than thinking and talking. People who plan design and construct frameworks where success can be obtained. They consider these questions:
1. What is the job?
2. What are the costs?
3. What are the risks?
4. What are the benefits?
5. Whose approvals are required?
6. Who is assigned to do the job?
7. When will processes commence?
8. What methods will be employed?
9. How will actions be reported?
10. To whom will the reporting occur?

11. How will successes or failures be evaluated?
12. Who will own processes and see them through to completion?

Planning without action doesn't produce deliverables. If action is commenced without sufficient planning, results may fall short of the excellence desired or required.

You've heard expressions used of people who don't plan: "He shoots from the hip," and "Ready, Fire, Aim!"

If an organization wants meritorious achievement it will leave very little to impulse, chance, or intuition. Great results are more readily secured when people plan.

Consider your team's desires and goals.
1. Plan well.
2. Act with excellence.
3. Report results.
4. Evaluate processes and products and celebrate ones that bear fruit in their term.

Products, in the long run, will be better in quality because a plan is decided and acted upon. Customer satisfaction will rise, as will your team's pride in their achievements, when you design action and follow through.

Lesson 42
Profit Centers

Are you profitable?

The term *profit* refers to monetary gain in excess of cost. It's what is retained after income is received and expenses are paid. Profit is considered the life blood of an enterprise when weighed against the costs of exchanging time and effort for dollars and cents.

Profit can be seen in other ways, too. For example, how profitable are you in the use of resources like energy and time? Do expenditures of these elements of success produce more than they cost? What remains when you balance income against output?

Profit is also evidenced in people. How are those who associate with you improved because of that connection? Or, how is what you invest into the people of your network helping you and them succeed?

Look at the worth of the individuals on your core teams and what they contribute. How profitable is production apart from them? How valued are persons when products alone become measures of worth?

Profit centers on that which is valuable and that which isn't, determined largely by what lasts, and what doesn't. Maturing people balance relationships and monetary rewards, intangible and tangible results.

Production and pecuniary outcomes occupy necessary places in business and it shall remain so. But people are more important and profitable than simply what they produce. How that lesson is understood and activated says much about how a firm views, uses, invests in, or abuses its networks. These networks include employees, employers, vendors, and customers.

Think about your customers. They are consumers and profit centers. How does your organization view and treat them? Are they handled as means to monetary wealth, or as persons into whom your team pours health, or both?

Giving and receiving are parts of the same transaction—both are profitable. When business is viewed and conducted with this fact in mind several important truths emerge:
1. Profit includes monetary gains.
2. Profit should be realized from expenditures of energy and time.
3. Profit resides in persons that are worth more than what they contribute or consume, because people are more important than production.
4. Profit is revealed in worthwhile investments and their outcomes. Investments in money making vehicles

should produce positive returns. Investments in lives should produce living legacies.
5. You are worth more than what you do.

Consider your profit centers, including your people and their production. Which are more valuable and why? How would you realign your value system to include people and production as profitable in multiple ways?

Lesson 43
Principles in Practice—Where Rubber Meets Road

Principles of truth become practices in life when behaviors improve. Leaders know this. Further, leaders model accountability and preferred behavioral change before requiring these alignments from those who follow.

Altering behavior is not easy. If a leader wants to build duplicative legacy, he or she takes initiative and turns valued principles into viable actions. Followers evaluate and emulate the model the leader provides.

Leadership for many is made up of power and position, domination and control. Leadership for those who exercise impact, influence, and investment is about modeling, motivating, caring, and sacrifice. If you were the follower, which would you rather have demonstrated?

While it might be easier for a leader to tell and not show, it isn't right. Lasting and effective leadership begins when the one leading engages in actions that reflect greater causes and project better outcomes.

If your followers are not exercising behaviors that you and your core team deem to be desirable, ask yourself: What behaviors will I change to show my team what I want and how to achieve it? When will I start?

Declaring and acting on positive decisions are signs of growth in a maturing individual. Behavioral change originates from the leader who cares, who understands that actions, not just words, are where traction occurs and destinations are reached.

Lesson 44
Without Decisive Action, It's Worthless

"We need..." is a common phrase. It is overused almost to the point of disgust in election campaigns. It's repeated on the job, too. Unfortunately, it is used in business meetings and conversations far too often.

In the final analysis the phrase is worthless unless plans and actions are attached to an idea. The next time you hear or say, "We need..." consider these questions:

1. Who is *we*?
2. What is the need?
3. Whom does the need affect?
4. Who will benefit from its resolution or fulfillment?
5. Who will own solving problems by creating a plan of action?
6. To whom will the plan be presented and when?
7. Who will approve the plan?
8. What is the budget and how will the project be funded?
9. Who will lead the action, build the team, and see the processes through?
10. Who will issue progress reports, how often, and to whom?
11. What is the expected delivery date?

12. When will the team or responsible party know that completion has occurred?
13. Who will evaluate and correct mistakes?
14. How will victories be celebrated?
15. When will we start to fulfill this need?

"We need..." is ineffectual because it leaves the parties who hear or articulate the phrase without much more than wishful thinking and surface conversation. Contemplation and completion are not the same. Unless action follows, the phrase is worthless.

Discussions without decisions and dedicated activities may address perceived or real deficiencies that beg for solutions. But when deliberations don't include job descriptions, role definitions, assignments, ownership, accountability structures, specific actions, faithfulness to duty, communication, closure, and evaluations, they're just conversations.

People who identify opportunities or problems are usually composed of two groups:
1. Those who identify a need and talk about it
2. Those who identify a need, discuss it, then decide, act, and produce effectual, verifiable results

Consider the team you lead or serve on. If you had a dollar for every "We need..." phrase you've heard or spoken in the last three weeks, how much extra money would be in your wallet?

What would it take to implement positive action steps the next time the phrase comes up? Try this: Design and distribute a list of questions like the ones above, stating that whenever someone utters a "We need..." they must be prepared with answers. Soon, very soon, people will think twice about bringing up a "We need..." without conducting reliable research, offering specific recommendations, and outlining plans for action and follow-up.

Discussions about issues must occur in open atmospheres that encourage creative thinking. Business communication requires this activity. Meetings and deliberations are important. Just remember to include assigned ownership and specific action to get needs fulfilled because apart from these the words alone carry little weight.

Lesson 45
Absentee Leadership

Great and strong leadership is present and accountable. Conversely, when a leader abandons his or her post a leadership vacuum is generated and it longs to be filled. Leadership vacancy is a sure sign that the one in charge is not making decisions about followers' successes.

Absentee leadership assumes multiple forms. Examples are physical, emotional, mental, or figurative and all of them share similarities.

When physically absent, a leader is simply gone, removed. There are times when not being present is unavoidable, of course—scheduling may require this. But as a character trait, it is simply a preference. People decide where to place themselves for what they consider the greatest good to be. The objective of their placement will benefit themselves, the people they lead, or both. If you are the leader, how present are you for your team and how do they know?

Leadership can be emotionally absent, too. A leader who doesn't desire to connect with his or her followers checks out, engaging in isolationism, silo-dwelling, or stove-piping. This leader's agenda promotes self above team and doesn't want to be bothered. This agenda prefers secrecy and hidden details.

Closely related to emotional absenteeism is mental disconnect. A leader who is mentally absent may not be suffering from psychological disorders. In the meaning intended here, he or she willfully chooses to ignore followers because of an "I could care less about other people" attitude born of self-absorption. This selfish person demonstrates a profound lack of interest in the welfare (right standing) of the team.

Figurative vacuums result when mediocre leaders refuse to make time or take interest in helping followers succeed. This absenteeism, no matter its form, puts function before relationship, people beneath production. It ultimately fails to promote anything but distance. It shuts down communication, avoids interaction, and lives in unrealistic expectations. Figurative absence is recognized in disconnected and disparaging attitudes and actions.

Engaged leaders are caring individuals who want their teams to win. They understand and promote interactive connection. They take initiative to provide it. These leaders understand and weigh superior options: how close to get, what styles of management to employ, how to avoid overbearing stances, when to request permission to "invade" a follower's space for their benefit, when to openly confront negatives, how to instruct, how to evaluate, and how to celebrate. Engaged leadership requires thought, time, energy, and other resources. It is far more focused on the welfare of the follower than the comfort of the leader.

Is the cost of engaged leadership worth it if you are the leader? How important is your team to you? Your presence or absence answers these questions. Your team hears, responds to, and emulates what they observe.

Lesson 46
When Followers Take Initiative

Taking initiative is a hallmark of leaders and followers who make positive differences on core teams. Initiative-taking is not personality driven nor is it position driven. It comes from desires to see a team succeed. The initiative taker creates environments of productivity into which other team members contribute.

Great leaders enjoy teaching and promoting growth in their followers. They are particularly gratified when followers take initiative born of personal desires for improvements or completion of tasks. Taking initiative is a sign of developing health and maturity.

When followers become initiative-takers, they become leaders in their own right, and this is right. A great leader promotes this growth for people who serve with him or her. Superior leadership also teaches that when followers take initiative their ideas must receive leadership's full approval before action commences.

How often do your followers offer creative ideas for your consideration as opposed to leaning solely on you for answers to perplexing issues, business requirements, or on the job duties? How often do your followers approach you with solutions to problems that need to be addressed, instead of dumping their difficulties on you?

The more your followers create and initiate, the better your leadership is transferred into the hearts, heads, and hands of those who assume task fulfillment. When followers take initiative they come to you with well thought out opportunities and solution options. Their initiative and your buy in make your team run better and promote collective wins.

Lesson 47
Leading From the Middle

You are an employee, perhaps a supervisor or middle manager, but not the boss. Or, perhaps you have no one working for you.

Let's say you clearly see needs for change, positive alterations you are convinced would help your organization improve product delivery, customer satisfaction, team cooperation, or leadership. Because you are not the one in charge, is it possible to affect healthy change? Is leading from the middle or from somewhere underneath the top a realistic expectation and, if so, how is it done?

Leading from the middle is tough but it is possible. It's tough because:
- Few people want to risk negative consequences if what they're proposing is rebuffed or refused from someone above them.
- The one with the ideas must prove that the ideas are worthy of consideration in the first place.
- The change agent needs to be reliable and authentic.

Leading from the middle can be done. When the person initiating fresh ideas demonstrates through words and works that his or her contributions are valuable and worth considering, leading from the middle occurs.

And there's the key. Leading from below the top is not accomplished in a vacuum. It's a result of the person who desires improvement producing ongoing excellence in his or her work ethic and delivery. Where an employee identifies needs for change and fails as a contributing force for good, conversations about change can be perceived as little more than complaining.

But where an employee demonstrates consistent contribution in task completion, that employee earns the right and responsibility to be heard by those who may sincerely welcome recommendations for needful and positive change. In short, proof encourages reception.

What changes would you like to see your organization employ that you are convinced would benefit its people and operation? How well do your work contributions demonstrate stability and accountability, giving you the platform or voice to recommend and implement the changes you desire?

It's always timely to begin a process of authentic and accountable contribution. This renders your opinions about needful change as viable and valuable. Show what you want before suggesting what you think your company needs.

Lesson 48
Problem Solving Techniques

In Chapter 10 of *Core Teams Work,* 21 core issues for core teams are listed and discussed. One of these is "Problem solving and solution-based thinking." Effective leaders understand the marked differences between whining and winning. They encourage and model the latter.

"People who are problem solvers think and act from positions of strength because they are committed to improvement. You know you have a greatness-empowered core team when the members see challenges as opportunities and confront negatives with positives." (Page 192)

Maturing leaders long to work with growing people. They teach problem-solving techniques to dedicated team members through words and actions. Leaders and followers cooperate to achieve desired outcomes.

How do you approach solving problems with your team? If team members aren't solution-based thinkers, then one of your responsibilities is to educate them on better ways of resolving difficult issues.

Consider teaching them the five problem solving stages as defined in *Leadership Is—*, pages 76-78.

1. Discover the *common ground* of interest and engagement. Recognize felt need. Identify real need.
2. Engender agreement on the *common good*. Articulate what is desired for resolution.
3. Agree on a *common goal*. This stage is where behaviors start to change.
4. Produce and share *common gains*. Coaching and encouragement are required along with actions that prove people are serious about solving issues.
5. Generate *uncommon results*. This state of problem solving is remarkable because most groups don't progress this far to realize their desired ends.

A leader is responsible to see that problems are solved by constructing frameworks in which resolutions can occur. In any organization the opportunity (or challenge!) of making sure problems are creatively addressed is a daily reality.

Tired, old, struggling, and frustrating styles of dealing with problems are discouraging and accomplish little. Where leaders endlessly tolerate unresolved issues, watch them implode or explode, try to please everyone, and probably endure voluminous episodes of whimpering and whining, they are operating out of failure at worst or frustration at least. These are never preferred ways to address negative issues.

L.E.A.D. — LEARNING, EDUCATION, ACTION, DESTINY

Do problem solving better. Create environments where ownership of responsibility is shared by people tasked to fulfill resolution. Develop a solution provision mindset that identifies common ground, common good, common goals, and common gains. Results will be remarkable as the processes come to term.

Foster shared responsibility, accountability, and faithfulness. Positive changes don't just happen when problems need to be faced. Preferred methods have to be taught, encouraged, modeled, and reinforced.

Leadership wants those who follow to take initiative, embrace problem resolution, obtain approval for the solutions they present, and perform problem solving well. Techniques are effective when they are instructed and implemented from dedicated leaders. When followers own solutions to problems they would otherwise present to leadership to solve, this team is winning.

Lesson 49
How Leaders Handle Discouragement

Yes, it happens to the boss. The assumption is that the leader stays tough, offering vision and direction, while avoiding visible signs of the intense internal battles discouragement brings.

Inward conflicts for leaders may be different in scope from those experienced by followers. But leaders get discouraged like everyone else, sometimes even more so. It comes with the territory from being on the front line, from thriving in spite of unmet or unrealistic expectations, when losses occur, when appreciation is absent, or when problems appear to be overwhelming (because sometimes they are).

Working through discouragement requires making deliberate choices and acting on them. Leaders move on principle when discouragement strikes. Consider:
1. Identify origins, the incidents (events or symptoms) and the issues (reasons or causes behind events). Dwell less on incidents and more on issues. Not focusing on symptoms alone shows maturity and wisdom. Dealing with tough central issues not only solves situations now; it may be preparation for greater problem resolution in the future.
2. Take a broader view. Evaluate how much importance

to attach to discouragement. Some circumstances are not worth the leader's time. Concentrate on the bigger issue items—smaller ones may be resolved when you do.

3. Align perspectives with values that endure. Eternal principles are just that, eternal. The "Law of Sowing and Reaping" (what one sows is what one reaps) and the "Law of Compensation" (payment will come, regardless) are reliable. See sources of discouragement from a return-on-investment point of view. Are the origins bad seeds in bad soil? Are they recompenses for wrong decisions? Or are these really minor mistakes, the results of which will soon pass into oblivion? What better investments could you make that would assure more lasting and positive returns?

4. Look realistically at assets and liabilities. What is working for and against you? Who are your supporters and detractors? What kinds of communication do you exercise with those who listen? How important is trying to communicate with those who don't listen? What information pathways could you construct to reduce mistakes and promote accuracy?

5. Focus on what you want instead of what you don't want. This purposeful choice yields refreshed perspectives.

6. Show followers how you face discouragement. Help them with theirs. Victory resides in processes, not just ends. Appropriately including others as you confront discouragement matures you and those you lead.

7. Forgive the past and move through pain. Perhaps not easily done, but necessary. Receive nourishment and encouragement from those you trust.
8. Create actions today that position improved results tomorrow. Put the laws of sowing, reaping, and compensation to work for you. Invest now for what you want then.
9. Choose positive attitudes and construct values-based decisions.
10. Replace negatives with the firm resolve that brought you to leadership's responsibilities in the first place.
11. Don't deny your feelings. Use them as motivators to go through, conquer, and perhaps alter circumstances that brought on the discouragement.
12. Become better for the journey. Those who follow will improve, too.

Discouragement is a natural occurrence. It comes and goes. It ebbs and flows. When it strikes, a great leader refuses to give up or cave in. This leader moves through and becomes better for the experience, because that's what committed leaders do.

L.E.A.D. — LEARNING, EDUCATION, ACTION, DESTINY

Lesson 50
Winning or Whining—What Do You Encourage?

Great leaders are solution thinkers and providers. They certainly aren't whiners. People who wallow and complain about problems fail to provide positive examples of resolution, even though they may be leading.

How do you face difficult circumstances or tough issues on your core team? Do you set a model of winning or whining?

Winners design and implement solutions. Whiners produce unobtrusive noise that accomplishes nothing.

Chapter 2 of *Industrial Strength Solutions* is titled "Winning vs. Whining." The big differences between these two attributes are discussed on pages 47-51. Bottom line: Winning happens when solutions are created. Whining disappears when a team refuses to give obsessive attention to negatives.

Four solution-thinking decisions accompany winners (see pages 51-57 of *Industrial Strength Solutions*):
1. Turn habits of complaining into habitats of construction. This is hard decision making from committed people.
2. Replace negative attitudes with positive solution-

focused outlooks. Decide and act on what you want, not what you don't want.
3. Redirect an ego-centered focus to concentrating on benefiting others. It is difficult to complain when offering assistance from a pure motive.
4. Confront problems with positive planning and action steps. Planning and acting for better results prove dedication and go a long way toward solving problems.

Win, don't whine. Your followers will respond to your leadership model. If you want to work with winners, teach your team what winning is through your example.

Lesson 51
Opportunities for Leadership Come From Circumstances and They Are Created

Opportunities to exercise great leadership come from circumstances and they are created as well. Great leaders don't just wait for right chances; they produce them.

The problems you and your team confront form environments in which positive results can be produced. This part of leading, seen in daily activity, is expected.

But if you want your team to grow beyond good and bad circumstances you may take reasonable risks to enhance learning. You may offer your people fresh opportunities for maturity they may not have contemplated, where they try new methods, compose fresh ideas, and create innovative scenarios. You will take initiative to teach them techniques of preparation and response. You want them to be ready.

Leaders stir the pot and light the flame knowing when they do that nothing will be the same. Not endeavoring to manufacture problems, leaders position their teams for readiness because leaders know that problems are sure to come.

Leaders who care take proactive stances and encourage growth, even if it's uncomfortable. Their focus is the positive development of the team. Their singular motivation is to help the team overcome odds and obstacles, prepare for the future, and mature while they do it.

Leaders strengthen their teams when they grow with them through good and bad circumstances. Leaders create environments of challenge to hone survival skills. Leaders help teams thrive beyond today. It's all about being ready no matter what comes your way.

Lesson 52
You Are More Important Than What You Do

You are valuable. As the leader you may be one of your business or group's most important and treasured resources. How do you view yourself and your leadership? Are you convinced you are more important that what you do, and that what you do is valuable?

At CTRG we offer our clients a needs assessment program called Relationship and Operational Structure Analysis (ROSA). We often say to clients who engage in ROSA that it takes a strong leader to go through it. Results, whether negative or positive, are laid at the doorstep of the leader. The one in charge owns causes and outcomes.

When needs for improvements are uncovered, a maturing leader takes responsibility to confront negatives. Effective leaders do not dwell in deficiency or fault-finding. Motivated leaders correct errors and move on, empowering followers to do the same thing.

Insecure leaders are not convinced that they are more important than their functional successes or failures. They question or deny that people are more important than what they do. These leaders may promote degradation on a team and practice relational disengagement. They may utilize tools that wound such as manipulation or intimidation. They may create isolationism by delegating tasks in a relational vaccuum. They may employ quick fixes to meet immediate need, ignoring or shunning the very people who could help them succeed.

Belief that people are more important than production, that relationships come before and give birth to function, must originate within leaders who want to expand what they know, who are not content with the status quo, who want to see their people grow. These leaders are the ones who convince themselves of their importance and worth and then pass those attitudes on to those they lead.

Leaders who earnestly desire team improvement agree on and adhere to growth of relationships *and* functions, focusing on building people *while* they increase production. This system takes longer to cultivate. It may require more time and resources to complete. But in the long run it's worth the expenditures. Principles last beyond temporary demands and heartless commands that too often characterize relationally vacuumed business environments. A wise leader builds on what endures, not what is expedient.

If you are the leader, recognize your inherent worth. You must start here. This recognition provides the foundation to affirm your followers and help them grow. They deserve this and so do you.

The strength of great leadership does not rest in title, power, position, or production, although these attributes have their place. The might and endurance of superior leadership resides in the character of the maturing and secure leader who gives himself or herself away for the benefit of followers, teaching them how to achieve greater works from the investments this leader makes.

It is to your and your company's best interests to build upon your organization's values, vision, mission, and message, your Code of Achievement. If your organization has not yet put these foundations in place, start the process immediately to identity and define them, ratify and implement them.

Values, vision, mission, and message provide proven strength in positive times and resilience when difficulties come. Commitments to invest in people today on the basis of values build guarantees of living legacies tomorrow no matter the circumstances. In or out of your organization, whether in your presence or absence, these resolutions and results endure.

Your goal is to become convinced that you and your team are more important than what you do. Internalize this truth for yourself, first. Earnestly present it to those who follow. Outcomes are sure for you and your team.

Closing

Reminders and resources are requisites in human experience. Commitments toward reaching positive life change are reinforced when endearing and enduring principles and practices are repeatedly brought to the forefront of thinking and acting.

Values compose a core team's skeleton truths, the foundations on which a healthy organization is built. A core team's vision, mission, and message rest upon its values. Upon these, their Code of Achievement, great teams contribute reliable words and responsible works.

L.E.A.D.—Learning, Education, Action, Destiny comprises a collection of leadership truths to read, a teaching tool to sow productive seed, and a reference manual to revisit in thought and deed. Use the book to empower your teams as you reinforce concepts and practices within yourself.

Learn, educate, and act upon one lesson every week of the year. This may be one method of involvement and investment that produces strengthened relationships and superior functions.

Live what you learn and teach. Your team's destiny will develop and legacy will form as you climb the mountain of principled leadership.

1. *Adapt* the lessons to your environment and teach them in your own words.
2. *Adopt* learned and life-altering behaviors into your experiences. Teach your team through words and examples. Create duplicative models as you engage with your followers.

Learn, educate, and act. Form a destiny that leaves a positive legacy of impact, influence, and investment. Processing new information and turning it into viable and verifiable living is a golden opportunity for people who want to grow. It is a worthy option for any leader who desires enduring results.

You are encouraged to heed what you read. You are empowered to grow and to L.E.A.D.

When will you begin? By what criteria will you measure gains, correct errors, and celebrate successes in yourself and your teams?

Acknowledgements

Individuals

Justin Aubrey, my son, in whom I am well pleased. He is a young man of many talents. In addition to working in the construction industry, he is a gifted artist in graphic design and classical drawing. He is the designer of the book and study guide's front and back covers.

Zela Aubrey, my mother, who at 92 years of age has contributed her memory of my early days and her sharpened perspective in support of my book writing efforts. What a treasure she is.

Jim DeMassimo, A&P, IA Cert., Director of Maintenance for a charter airline service in southern California. Jim is a professional resource in the airline industry. He graciously contributed his expertise regarding aircraft O-ring hydraulics.

Jeff Goble, one of the long-standing and faithful contributors to the success of CTRG. Jeff has been with our organization since the beginning. He serves us as webmaster, analyst, and editor. More importantly, he is a treasured friend. He is also one of the wittiest and most humorous people I have ever known.

Heather Hoffman, my daughter, who is a tremendous support in the CTRG office. She and her husband, Neil, work with teenagers through their church, encouraging young people to make better choices early in life. I am extremely proud of her.

Jordan Peck, my Executive Assistant at Creative Team Resources Group, Inc. (CTRG). She is a long-time friend of our family, a right arm in administration. She is also the acquisitions editor for Creative Team Publishing (CTP). Jordan is the best.

Art Williams, a long time friend, pilot, Army veteran, and professional musician. His encouragement and humor are gifts I have treasured for many years. His most recent contribution to me is seen in the O-ring illustration in Lesson 38.

Organizations

Creative Team Resources Group, Inc. (CTRG) and **Creative Team Publishing (CTP),** El Cajon, California. CTRG and CTP provide means to develop and present life-changing curriculum to leaders and core teams around the world. It's a privilege to work in these organizations.

Olive Garden Restaurant, Santee, CA. General manager Dennis Jenkins, hostess/greeter Theresa E. Aguilar, and certified trainer and service assistant Chris Tucker have consistently shown me to my favorite outside table (Siena #602) where much of the content of the first three business books was completed and many edited versions were reviewed and revised.

Ottavio's Restaurant, El Cajon, CA. This is where one of my "private offices" is located. I offer special thanks to Paul Donato, Melanie Luck, Grace Howerton, Nannette Oliver, and Karen Cox for their service and friendship. They have given me privacy and provision innumerable times.

Outback Restaurant, La Mesa, CA. Donald Jones, who has served me well and often manages this facility, continually provides space, smiles, and support of my writing endeavors. We are both students of following and leading.

L.E.A.D. — LEARNING, EDUCATION, ACTION, DESTINY

www.ctrg.com
www.LeadershipIs.com
www.IndustrialStrengthSolutions.com
www.CoreTeamsWork.com
www.Lead52.com
www.Lincoln-Leadership-Gettysburg.com

CTRG provides quality resources for the development of teams within organizations whose desires are to grow and develop their personnel and achieve greater results in product or service provision. CTRG gives people great information that allows them to make changes in how they live and work and does this through building core teams. Our resources include personnel training, seminars, counsel, one-on-one and small-group leadership coaching, books, and instruction manuals.

Our foundational principle is that people are more important than production and relationships precede and give definition to function. The value of a person's contributions comes from that person's inherent worth. The value of the person causes the contributions a person makes to achieve even greater results.

Contact CTRG at the websites above. We will demonstrate first-hand how our team building principles can work for you. Glen Aubrey, President and CEO, along with other CTRG staff are available to your group for speaking engagements, on-site training and leadership coaching. CTRG looks forward to serving and working with you!

The Author

Glen Aubrey is President and CEO of Creative Team Resources Group, Inc. (CTRG), www.ctrg.com. He is an author, business consultant, leadership trainer, conference speaker, professional musician, music writer and orchestrator, and poet. He has authored *Leadership Is—How to Build Your Legacy, Industrial Strength Solutions Build Successful Work Teams!, Core Teams Work Their Principles and Practices, Growing Core Teams, Core Team Impact!, Go From the Night, Arranging Notes, L.E.A.D.—Learning, Education, Action, Destiny,* and *Lincoln, Leadership and Gettysburg.*

You are invited to visit these websites:
www.ctrg.com
www.CreativeTeamPublishing.com
www.LeadershipIs.com
www.IndustrialStrengthSolutions.com
www.CoreTeamsWork.com
www.Lincoln-Leadership-Gettysburg.com
www.GoFromTheNight.com
www.Lead52.com
www.glenaubrey.com

The Publisher

Creative Team Publishing (CTP) is a division of Creative Team Resources Group, Inc. (CTRG, www.ctrg.com). CTP was formed in 2007 to publish and distribute business and team development, leadership training, and poetry books, as well as literature of inspiration, insight, human achievement, and positive general interest.

The company's commitment is to make high quality literature available and engage in excellence throughout the process of publication. Customer satisfaction is a top priority. Because CTP practices due diligence in selecting which books it will publish, CTP chooses to work with customers who meet a qualified standard of literary competence and uplifting content.

CTP is a fee-for-service publisher. Products offered include the following:

Pre-Press
1. Editing
2. Proofing
3. Revision
4. Typesetting
5. Four Color Cover Design
6. ISBN
7. Print Set-up

Post-Press
1. Product supply
2. Press releases

Contact Creative Team Publishing. Please visit our company website, **www.CreativeTeamPublishing.com**, for information. We look forward to reviewing your literary creation.

GLEN AUBREY

Products

Books and Curriculum by Glen Aubrey
Available through Creative Team Resources Group, Inc.
Online Store
www.ctrg.com

Leadership Is— How to Build Your Legacy

Industrial Strength Solutions Build Successful Work Teams!

Core Teams Work Their Principles and Practices

Lincoln, Leadership and Gettysburg

Go From the Night

L.E.A.D.—Learning, Education, Action, Destiny

Growing Core Teams

Core Team Impact!

Arranging Notes

L.E.A.D. — LEARNING, EDUCATION, ACTION, DESTINY

Music CD Recordings by Glen Aubrey
Available through Creative Team Resources Group, Inc.
Online Store
www.ctrg.com

Beautiful, A Symphonic Experience
Music by Lindamarie Todd and Glen Aubrey

Born Is the King
Christmas Keyboard Reflections
Piano solos

The Custom Album
Piano Solos by Glen Aubrey

Go From the Night Meditation
Glen Aubrey, Solo Piano
Pat Kelley, Guitars
Go From the Night Selected Readings

Meditation
Glen Aubrey, Solo Piano
Pat Kelley, Guitars

Reflecting Hymn
The Rock Album
Piano solos

What Child Is This
Glen Aubrey, Solo Piano

www.ingramcontent.com/pod-product-compliance
Lightning Source LLC
Chambersburg PA
CBHW022013290426
44109CB00015B/1157